D0993286

WITHDRAWN

WP 0824654 8

PRACTICAL

CHILDREN

Dancing

CHILDREN
Dancing

Rosamund Shreeves

Second edition

UNIVERSITY OF WOLVERHAMPTON LIBRARY	
Acc No. 824654	CLASS
CONTROL	372 . 86 SHR OS
DATE 23. FEB. 1993	SITE WL

Ward Lock Educational Co. Ltd.

WARD LOCK EDUCATIONAL CO. LTD.
1 CHRISTOPHER ROAD
EAST GRINSTEAD
SUSSEX RH19 3BT
UNITED KINGDOM

A MEMBER OF THE LING KEE GROUP
HONG KONG · SINGAPORE · LONDON · NEW YORK

© Ward Lock Educational Co. Ltd.
All rights reserved. No part of this publication may be reproduced, stored
in a retrieval system, or transmitted in any form or by any means,
electronic, mechanical, photocopying, recording or otherwise,
without the prior written permission of the Publisher.

Text © Rosamund Shreeves 1979,1990

First published – 1979
Second edition – 1990
Reprinted – 1991, 1992

ISBN 0-7062-4988-7

Printed in Hong Kong

Dedication

To my Father
Full Circle

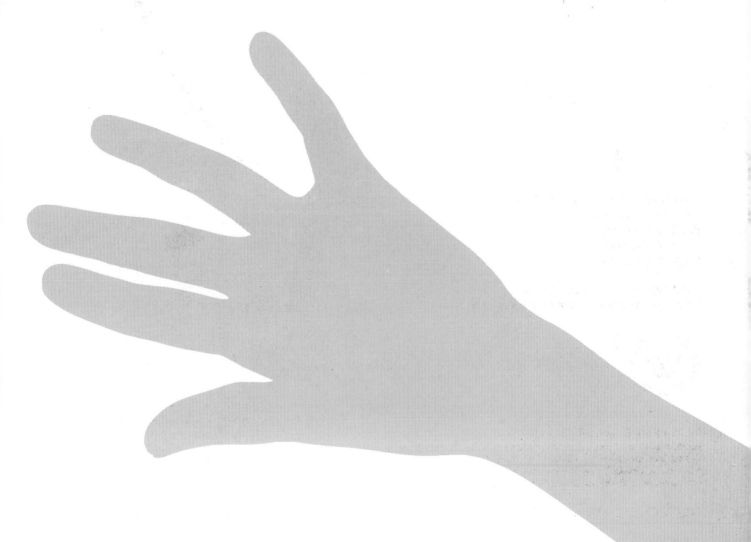

Acknowledgements
The author would like to thank the following:
Annie Williams and the children from Christchurch Primary School,
London W1
Lynn Harnan and the children from Hogarth Junior School,
London W4
The children from Ecton Brook Middle School,
Northampton
The children from Norwood Green Infant School,
Hounslow, Middlesex
John Auty, Dance Inspector for ILEA.

Contents

Part 1

General

Movement Content

The Lesson

Starting Activities

Exploring and Developing Movement

The Dance

Accompaniment

Part 2

Ideas for Dance

Flash Cards

Movement Patterns

Objects

Dressing Up

People

Moods and Emotions

Animals

Nature

Part 3

The Example Lessons

Imagery and Action Words

Movement Patterns

Objects

Dressing Up

People

Moods and Emotions

Animals

Nature

Seasonal Events

Shapes

Sound

Poetry

Pictures

Colourful Locations

Machines

Games

Ocean

Appendices

Preface

Dance in schools must be seen within the context of dance in society.

The past ten years or so have seen a growing relationship between dance and mime and the education profession. Dance groups, solo artists and companies have offered an educational service through workshops, residencies and performances. Much valuable experience has thus been gained on both sides, and the gaps of understanding between the performing world and the education world are beginning to close. Often the relationship is not an easy one and problems have to be recognized and overcome, but there is an enormous potential for enrichment within it. Many schools nowadays are using professional dancers as a resource and out of this liason much exciting work has arisen. New ideas are brought about by working *together*.

Although in danger from financial cuts and recent retrograde thinking, dance in schools is now more widely recognized as being for girls *and* boys, for older and younger children and for those with special needs. Dance can be seen as a vehicle for expressing concerns and beliefs, as a powerful vehicle for human expression.

In addition, the huge growth in the interest in and provision for community dance, particularly through the efforts of the dance animateurs, has helped to demystify dance and make it more accessible to everybody, regardless of sex, age, race or ability. More people are now choosing and having access to the sort of dance they want, whether it is as participants or as audience. There is now a greater variety of spaces and places *where* dance takes place — in parks, galleries, fashion shows, hospitals, in prisons, in the streets, on beaches — as well as more traditionally in halls, arts centres and theatres.

The barriers between the different forms of movement are breaking down. The sharp dividing lines between dance as an art, as a social activity, as a ritual or for health are blurring. There are many more different forms of movement and dance which have influenced the dance scene, for example, T'ai Chi, Aikido, Contact Improvisation, Massage, Afro Caribbean, Asian dance and Alexander Technique. New Dance artists are evolving work from a range of skills.

This inevitably affects dance in schools which, in turn, feeds ideas into society. Interest in the relationships between the arts has extended the links between dance and music and involved the visual arts and language. Schools can be wonderful places to explore and use these connections, and also to provide bases for inter-community arts. Children now have more opportunity (although not nearly enough) to see dance in a wider context. This can be a great stimulus for creativity.

Against this background, *Children Dancing*, essentially a practical book, will be of use within many of these contexts and within any type of school or community group. Underlying these ideas is my belief in the joy and value of dance, not only for the individual but also for society. Growth is impossible without change. I believe that we must be open to change, that we must be sensitive to embryonic thoughts and imaginings, without which there is no progress. Each dance lesson can be a time for deepening awareness and discovery.

R. O. Shreeve.

'We have to bear in mind . . . the changing nature of life and work which lies before young people. . . . we need young people with imagination and commitment to drive events to a fruitful conclusion.'

From *Dance Education and Training in Britain* a report by the Calouste Gulbenkian Foundation.

Part 1

General

1 Introduction

Making dance is as valid as making music or making stories. Although dance enriches many other activities, it does not need to be justified in any terms other than itself. Dance is a truly unique and direct form of communication, rooted deep in our physical and emotional selves. Movement is our earliest means of expression. Our bodies respond with movement far more instinctively than with words. But too often this non-verbal use of ourselves is not recognized or lies dormant.

Many people nowadays are rediscovering the need to dance and the happiness this brings them. Dance is a unifying activity involving the whole self. It is both disciplined and spontaneous. The experience of dance involves simultaneously feeling, imagination and thought with the consequent increasing awareness and ability in all these areas. To dance is in the deepest sense of the word to *be* more vividly. Self-awareness grows with movement awareness.

Curt Sachs writes about the need to dance as 'an effervescent zest for life'. This children certainly have. In dance, many children experience release and satisfaction not found in any other activity

Dance can spring from anything in human experience. The basis of dance is broad and far-reaching, but the *expression* is always in terms of movement. Rhythmic movement is the raw material of dance: the rhythms arise out of the movement and the impulse to dance. A dancer uses rhythms and shapes in the same way that a painter might use colours and textures.

Dance is concerned with evolving rhythms and patterns of movement which can symbolize or represent human activity. In this way it is different from mime or drama.

2 Description of the Book

The book is intended as a practical guide to the teaching of creative dance to children. Part 1 describes movement content, i.e. what to dance about and methods of working. Part 2 shows how movement content can be related to a wide variety of ideas. Part 3 is a collection of lessons exemplifying Parts 1 and 2. They are intended as detailed examples of both movement materials and methods of working. Some suggestions for 'follow-up' work in different media are included in this section.

The movements and examples are deliberately simple. Action words drawn from everyday language are used to communicate and stimulate movement. It is hoped that the visual effect of the action words will help the teacher to 'feel' the rhythm and quality of the movement herself.

The book is not intended as a comprehensive study of movement, but as an indication of a way of working. Basic movement concepts are developed and repeated throughout the book, giving plenty of opportunity for assimilation and repetition. Directed movement examples go alongside creative work in order to encourage both bodily skills and movement imagination.

It will be evident that there is much cross-sectioning of ideas. Any one idea could invariably be linked to another, so the teacher may need to read several sections to clarify her thoughts. The numbering throughout should facilitate this. Where relevant, music, poetry, reference books and follow-up activities are mentioned in the text.

The book need not be read straight through. Some may find it easier to read a few lesson examples and then refer back to the general heading in Parts 1 and 2.

3 Aims

To encourage:
  body awareness and sensitivity
  movement flow
  physical and emotional fitness
  creativity in movement and thought
  response to the surrounding environment.

In other words, to relate meaningfully to anything in the child's environment or experience, and to encourage similar ways of working in other media.

4 The Teacher

The teacher provides specific movement ideas. She is both instigator and guide, and she plans the lesson so that the children have an opportunity to become deeply involved in a variety of movement. It is essential to *plan* in advance both the movement and the sort of accompaniment that is to be used. On the other hand, it is equally important to remain open to suggestion, to seize the moment, to listen and to allow starting points and development to come from the children as well. Trust in children's response and allowing them their *own* experience of the movement are essential.

In each lesson the teacher may direct many of the movement phrases, both to ensure that a movement is fully experienced and also to give models on which variations may be built. The balance between freedom and imposition is only achieved after much practice. Dance is essentially a 'doing' activity with creative interaction between teacher and children. (*See also* **22**.)

The Teacher

Suggests

observes

listens

joins in

responds

guides

5 Involvement and Interaction

The teacher must be fully involved with the movement and the children. It is through sensitive interaction in suggesting, observing, guiding and responding that dance teaching takes place. This is not always easy, but movement generates energy. To become involved is to become refreshed. The teacher does not have to dance fully (she can use her hands and voice), but she must in the early stages be feeling with, not standing back and observing. There is a place for that later on when the children are more experienced and secure.

The ability to dance well oneself does not necessarily denote a good dance teacher. Use *your* own skills and sensitivities to guide children towards expressive, clear and formulated movement. You do not have to be predictable and follow a set format each time. Change is of the essence in dance. This book provides a simple basis of ideas; using this as a starting point, the teacher's knowledge and awareness can grow alongside that of the children.

6 Excitement

Children who are fully involved in movement will be excited in the sense of being enlivened. To dance is to move more precisely and more fully than in everyday life. Movements are repeated for the enjoyment of the rhythmic sensation. Vitality and energy are aroused. The child's sense of his whole being is heightened.

Unless the teacher gives clear movement directives, and fully involves the children, their energy becomes purposeless and they lose concentration. This is what sometimes happens and teachers then lack confidence to repeat the lesson. It is important to state clearly when the children are to begin *moving* and when they are to *stop*. (The muscular experience of stillness is as important as that of moving.) She can also state clearly whether they are to move *on the spot* (in place) or *travel* about the room. Conversely, if the teacher does not fully involve the children, lethargic action and inattention can result.

7 Movement as the Keynote

Sometimes teachers will rely on story and mimetic movement as they feel these may hold the children's attention better; however, it is the excitement of the story and not of the movement that does so. In dance, it is the movement ideas themselves which must generate enthusiasm and make the children want to react.

Focusing

Encourage *concentration* on the body and the physical sensation of the movement. Of course, words are useful for the initial communication but it is important to encourage *non-verbal* participation. Ask the children to 'show me with your bodies, not your voices'. Be aware of the inner non-verbal nature of dance.

Only through *focusing* on the physical sensation and feeling in their movement and their bodies do children achieve that state of personal involvement from which creativity springs and which is beautiful to observe.

Flow

Help children to feel a *flow of movement* in their bodies so that they move with ease and a sense of connection from one movement to the next. Flow encourages the rhythmic element that tends to release creativity. It is very much concerned with a *sense* of weight and momentum. If the body is held too tightly, the joints and muscles are inhibited from moving freely. There is less body sensation. A 'tight' body does not 'feel' so much and therefore is less able to move with ease and subtlety of expression. (*See also* **13** *and* **25**.)

Awareness through touch

Our awareness of ourselves is affected all the time by our environment. We feel cold, warmth, hardness, softness and our bodies respond accordingly. We learn about shape, proximity, textures, etc., not just through our eyes but through our tactile sense.

Encourage children to be aware of physical contact with their surroundings and with each other. For example:
Sitting — feel your contact with the floor, which parts of you touch the floor. Rock gently and slowly from side to side in this sitting position.

Standing — feel the floor under your feet and spread out your toes like a fan. Then wriggle them about as if the floor is sand.
Lying — roll very slowly from position to position. Feel the floor, touching your back, your stomach, your head. Roll very softly. Let the floor hold you. (*See also 25 and 26.*)

The teacher can use touch to intensify a movement idea. For example:

1 Stroke up the spine to suggest lengthening.
2 As the head hangs forward, stroke down the neck and head to encourage 'letting go', feeling the weight of the head.
3 Press gently on top of the shoulders to release hunched shoulders.
4 Use touch creatively as a *cue* to begin moving or stop.

Encourage the use of objects and fabrics to move with.

Make touching and being sensitive to others around a part of the dance experience. Something as simple as joining hands in a circle can be a structured and focused experience. Encourage children to be careful with each other and notice what their partner is doing as well as themselves. Tell them to move gently, not to 'bump' before trying more vigorous forms of contact.

Awareness through Mind Pictures
As well as connecting movement ideas to parts of the body, try deepening awareness of body parts by dwelling on mind pictures about the body. Use images and colourful language to create an inner picture of how the body looks and feels. These mind pictures will increase sensitivity and awareness.

A spine picture
Sit very still with your back straight. Imagine the very bottom of your spine. Then imagine all the way up your spine right up to your skull. Imagine your spine growing in the very centre of your body. Breathe out and let your spine and head bend forwards towards the ground. Sit up and let your spine think how it wants to move.

> stretch and wriggle
> bend and shake.

A head picture
Imagine your head is floating, just attached by a string to your body. Imagine your head is full of air and very light, so light it is floating upwards. Imagine a light floating colour inside your head. Let your head move gently.

Find some more mind pictures for different parts of your body.

Children are very responsive to these mini-meditations, especially if you ask them for feedback afterwards. Movement can follow these moments of thought. (*See also 27 and 55-57.*)

8 Voice to Accompany

The use of the voice is very important. The teacher can suggest *what* the children are to do and, by using the voice expressively, can communicate *how* they are to do it. The teacher's voice is in one sense 'doing' the action the children are experiencing. Just to say 'walk' or 'stretch' will not communicate the essential nature of the action and the children may move with little involvement. The voice can be the rhythmic accompaniment to the action and it is the rhythmic content of movement that involves and vitalizes. For example, draw out the word:

s - t - r - e - t - c - h !

making sure that the children are really extending as far as they can. Or use a firm rhythmic and accented quality in the words:

Walk, walk, walk and *turn*!

Say the words or make voice sounds. Use the voice in any way to make the movement flow in phrases.

9 Percussion to Accompany

Playing a percussion instrument is another useful way of communicating. We can all learn to play simple movement rhythms.

Play the instrument to indicate when to move and when to be still. The children can move to the sound of the instrument and stop when the instrument stops or vice versa, i.e. move in the silence after the instrument has sounded like a movement echo to the sound. The instrument can indicate the rhythm and nature of the action, showing whether, for example, it is a large, strong action or a quick, light one. Tap quickly and lightly and stop for:

> Run, run, run, run, run, run and balance!

The use of percussion is indicated in many of the lesson examples. (*See also* **48-53**.)

Find different ways of playing percussion instruments which will correspond to different types of actions. For example, a drum can be banged, tapped, smoothed, played loudly or softly.

Make repetitive sound patterns to suggest different ways of moving. Give enough time to establish the sound pattern and the movements it provokes. Children can take it in turns to play a pattern for the rest of the class to respond to.

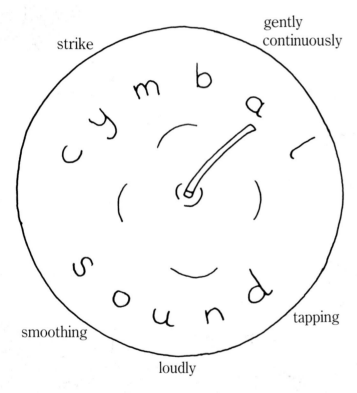

strike

gently
continuously

smoothing

tapping

loudly

for turning, rising, rolling
foot work, leap
expanding
balance
fall, still

Movement Content

10 An Analysis

No matter what the idea for the dance may be, it is the opportunities for movement and the logical development of that movement which determine the course of the lesson.

There are many ways of looking at movement and everyone will see it differently according to their background and perceptions. It is important to link the following ideas to *your* way of looking. What do *you* see as you look at dance? It is essential to *look* at children's movement because it is from your observations and from theirs that the dance material progresses.

Just as we might look at a painting and first get an overall impression and subsequently become aware of shapes, colour, etc., so in movement we can look more closely at the material presented. Any human movement will have certain things in common. It will be concerned with:

> the body
> actions
> qualities of movement
> space and relationships.

Movement can be defined in these terms by asking:

> What parts of the body are involved?
> (whole body, shoulders, back, fingers, eyes, etc.)
> What is the action?
> (rising, turning, stretching, walking, etc.)
> What is the quality of the action (how you move)?
> (fast, slow, staccato, weighty, flowing, etc.)
> Where does it go in the space?
> (Up, down, forwards, etc., through a variety of body shapes.)

In addition, we can observe *relationships* between one part of the body and another and between partners, groups, objects and the surrounding environment.

Of course, all these aspects will not appear to be evident simultaneously but they provide a starting point for looking at movement. For example, we might observe:

> A flowing dance going down to the floor and up again with wide movements and clear changes of direction *or* a strongly rhythmic dance with very articulate use of the body and quick interplay with a partner *or* an action-packed dance full of rolling, spinning, balancing and leaping with dramatic stops and starts.

Using this analysis, action can be varied. (*See* **34-37**.) The following poem (from *Peepshow: A Little Book of Rhymes* by Pamela Blake) exemplifies the idea of varying a single action

> The High Skip
> The Sly Skip
> The Skip like a Feather
> The Long Skip
> The Strong Skip
> And the Skip All Together

11 Action Words

These can help define what the body or parts of the body are doing. The following is a list of words for movement and stillness. Throughout the book, there are many indications as to how the teacher can deepen the awareness of the action. The list includes all the basic ways of moving but is not meant to be definitive.

The action words act as catalysts in the creative situation: they start off movement invention. Words can be used as a basis for practising movement, becoming more skilful, and for creativity.

Dances can be made using action words as a basis. Begin by exploring single words in phrases of going and stopping. Then begin to link contrasting words together. See the illustration opposite. (*See* illustration on *page 82*.)

walk	stop	stamp	slither
run	settle	clap	slide
skip	freeze	jab	rush
gallop	hold	push	dodge
leap	pause	pull	zig-zag
hop	hide	smooth	dash
jump	listen	cut	dart
roll	look	shake	drift
crawl	balance	hit	float
bounce	hover	throw	skim
		whip	stride
		tap	glide
dive	open		fly
melt	close		whirl
flop	grip	explode	tip toe
fall	stretch	toss	
pounce	swing	shoot	
crumple	sway	reach	stand
duck	turn	rise	lie
plunge	twist	grow	kneel
shrink	arch	spread	
expand			

12 Understanding Action Words

Children may not be familiar with the action word. The true understanding of the movement and the word comes from 'doing' over and over again in different situations. The teacher may communicate the ideas through her hands, an object, a rhythm, or any of the many ways indicated in the book. Words can arise from movement and be used to define it. There is constant interplay between language and movement — the one enriches the other. Children become interested in words that describe their movement.

Young children spontaneously use words to accompany themselves and will suggest colourful words like 'swirling' or invent new ones like 'clumping'.

Dance a Word

s t r e t c h i n g
Imagine yourself getting longer as you stretch
Feel yourself lengthening

Rolling
Find out about slow rolling. Try rolling across your back on your knees, stretched out or curled up.
Pause and discover the position you are in.

13 Action Phrases

Phrases or sequences evolve naturally from a sense of which movements 'go together'. The growth of one movement to the next must be *felt* in the muscles. There is a difference between mere labelling and kinetic understanding. There is a movement logic which determines which movement follows what, and where in the space. Feel and observe what is happening.

Rather than the children talking about which movements will go together, encourage quick thinking at the moment of moving. Encourage trust in body language through discovering the 'words' that will arise. For example:

> Feel how the momentum of jumping *down* can empower the *leap* upwards *or* how letting the weight go in sinking down can lead into a soft roll and a stretch out on the floor *or* how the speed of a spin can lead into quick jumps and springs.

Help the flow of movement with the accompaniment. Give children sequences to practise and help them to discover their own phrases. Dance is about the *relationship* of one movement to the next, one rhythm to the next and one person to another.

Gradually encourage the children to build longer sequences and more 'aware' action where the body parts, shapes or rhythm are clear. The more skilful the child, the more he will be able to *link* actions together and also to *combine* actions, for example:

> linking—run and jump and fall
> combining—skipping with opening and closing the arms.

From an early age children delight in rhythmic phrases of dance. A four-year-old said:

> I can swing and move and dance
> I can swing and stretch and arch.

The movement arising need not be totally defined in terms of words, but words can help to clarify and define what is happening. (*See also page 82.*)

14 Variety

'To dance is to move . . . more fully than in everyday life'. Therefore children must be helped to feel the extremes of their movement, to feel the contrast of reaching out into the space and curling up small, to feel the release of leaping high and the contrast of moving low. Every lesson should contain contrasts and variety. Only the teacher can judge the length of time that should be allowed to develop a particular activity. Very young children tire quickly and need to work in short phrases of activity and rest.

Consider the action word list (*see 11*) in terms of contrast.

15 Going and Stopping Contrasts

In dance there is constant interplay between moving and stopping; different ways of moving, different ways of stopping; energy being expended and gathered again. Rhythm and phrasing in dance arise out of this muscular feeling of when to move and when to be still.

Stillness
Try to notice where pauses occur naturally within the phrase and draw the children's attention to them. A pause is often a preparation for a movement or a recovery from it. Ask questions:

> Where is your stillness?
> Make it clear in your body when you are moving, and when you are still.

It is often necessary to practise *feeling* stillness so link moving words with stopping words to make simple phrases of movement and accompany them on a percussion instrument, or with your voice. For example:

Running and balancing	Practise running lightly and easily, balancing and lifting the body, feeling the moment to run again.
Stride and freeze	Practise striding firmly, stopping firmly. Make a phrase through using a change of direction.
Skip and pause	A phrase of skipping, pause, and waiting to hear the accompaniment before skipping again.
Bounce and hide	Practise bouncing high and hiding (crouching) near the ground.
Stopping words, e.g.	freeze
	pause
	settle

These words encourage an awareness of different types of stopping. 'Look' helps the children to think ahead to where they are going to move next in space.

Make rhythms of going and stopping phrases. Repeat them over and over at one time so that the movement really 'gets going'. Find going and stopping contrasts on the action word list. (*See 11.*)

16 Body-part Contrasts

Movement contrasts can be demonstrated by using one part of the body after another, for example:

> the hands can clap
> the feet jump
> the arms swing

or by performing contrasting movements with one particular part. For example:

> the feet stamp, jump and slide.

Make lists of body-part action words. The children can make an enormous drawing of the body and label it with action words. Note how many of the actions can be performed by the whole body or part of the body.

Phrases of body-part action words can be practised in the classroom and in the movement lesson. Placing emphasis on different body parts makes the children *feel* them more vividly. Many of the 'lessons' stress movement of body parts.

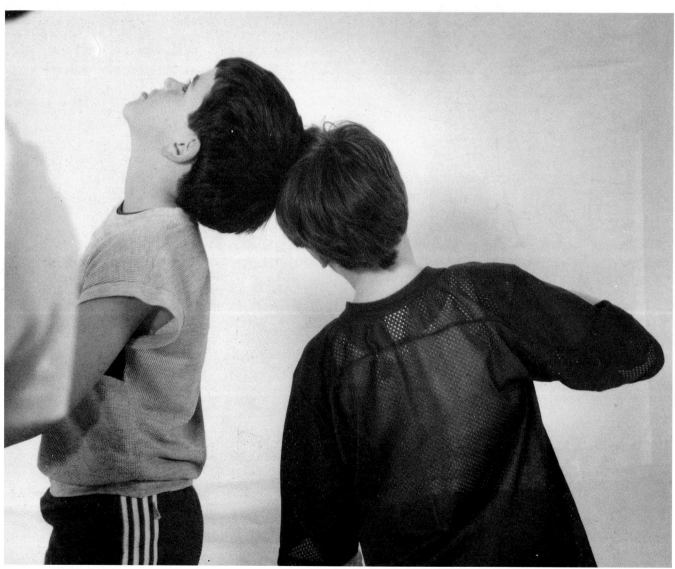

17 Qualitative Contrasts

Action words may stress the qualitative (the 'how?') aspect of movement and give a movement experience of, for instance, speed or slowness, strength or lightness. For example:

> glide
> explode
> rush
> crumple.

Use words to stimulate a more sensitive use of the body. The ability to move qualitatively will develop after much practice and repetition in many different dance situations.

The above actions might be practised by the whole body or a body part, for example:

glide — with the fingertips
(sitting) 'Bring your fingertips together so that they touch very gently. Let them glide away into the space, then come back and touch again gently.'

Many qualitative words arise from looking and touching, from poems and stories. Look at the action word list. (*See* **11**.)

18 Spatial Contrasts

Words can communicate spatial ideas too. Encourage *feeling* the space. For example, feel the difference between moving slowly backwards or rushing forwards or sinking down or shooting upwards. Contrast *travelling* movement with *in place* movements. Words like:

> leaping
> rolling
> skipping

are *travelling* words whereas:

> rising
> sinking
> stretching

suggest moving *in place*.

At the beginning of a lesson, movements in place often *involve* the children more successfully than travelling movements which need skill in avoiding and giving way to others.

Of course, any movement which travels along, like 'skipping', can be performed in place and a movement which begins in place like 'stretching' may develop into travelling. Other spatial contrasts involve change of *direction*:

> forwards
> backwards
> above
> around

and changes of *level*:

> high or low movements which contrast moving into the air or near the ground.

Encourage children to move fully in the space all around the body.

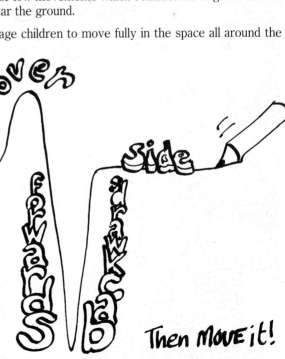

Make a drawing. Use the words to move to.

19 Relationship Contrasts

Try to vary in the lesson whether the children are dancing by themselves, with the teacher, or a partner. Help them to dance with others as well as alone. Make transient relationships at first. For example:

Turn to the person nearest to you and . . .
All face me and copy . . .
Point to someone far from you and . . .

Make it fun! Encourage moving with different partners.

20 A Diagram of Movement Contrasts

Of course no one lesson contains all contrasts! (See the suggested lessons in Part 3 for examples.) Contrasts ensure an ebb and flow of energy, a balance between activity and rest, high energy and calm. This balance in the lesson is far more important to the success of the lesson than any stimulus. A particular type of contrast might be stressed over a number of lessons.

Observe your children. See what sort of contrasts you think they need.

Young children on the whole enjoy cruder contrasts.

Later children develop more subtlety in their movement response.

Give children the opportunities to discover the many possibilities within their own bodies, to widen their scope for creative expression. Ways of moving are strongly rooted in our physical and emotional selves and are truly reflective of inner states. Through observing the children and presenting a wide variety of ideas, the teacher can help nourish and develop the qualities within each child.

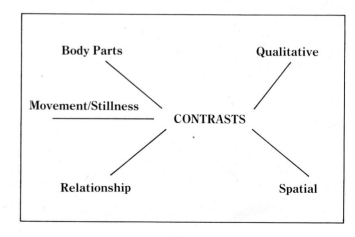

Body Parts   Qualitative

Movement/Stillness —— CONTRASTS

Relationship   Spatial

The Lesson

21 Planning the Lesson

The lesson is a creative situation. No two classes will be alike. The lesson examples in Part 3 are imaginary dialogues based on experience in similar situations. The aims of giving the children opportunity to both *practise* and *create* movement suggest the following lesson framework, the use of which will vary from teacher to teacher and situation to situation.

Each part of the lesson may be freely interwoven with another. Some lessons may be mostly directed with a little creative work towards the end. Some lessons may stress exploration in movement while others concentrate on making a dance; selecting and consolidating ideas. Whatever the stress, try to end with some corporate movement which

will draw everyone together with the feeling of being part of a group. With young children the culmination of the lesson might be a simple unison movement with the teacher. Older children enjoy making dances of their own which can be improved and added to over several weeks.

In planning the lesson consider:

1 *Starting activities* — to encourage concentration and body awareness and to improve movement skill. (*See* **24-33** for details.)
2 *Exploring and developing movement* — individual creativity. (*See* **34-38**.)
3 *Making a dance* — selecting an idea or ideas from the central part of the lesson and clarifying a beginning and ending. (*See* **39-47**.)
4 *Accompaniment.* (*See* **48-53**.)

22 A Lesson Example

The children sit near the teacher and work on some gentle preparatory exercises to involve them and focus attention, perhaps curving forward then arching their backs,

> stretching upwards,
> wriggling and loosening their spines,
> then sitting very still.

Link these activities to their breathing. They stand and in place practise stretching, swinging and jumping sequences; then travel about the room with big stretching upward leaps and crouch jumps downwards.

They breathe deeply and 'hang down', feeling their spines lengthening, their heads heavy.

Taking plenty of time they explore falling and rising to standing again as a movement idea. This leads to a variety of sequences and involvement with a partner.

They discuss feelings and thoughts which arise from this experience. They build short partner dances. Some give titles to their dance, for example, 'slow motion' or 'ambush'.

Throughout the lesson stress is laid on sensitive use of parts of the body both in their movement and in their contact with the floor.

The lesson is finished in a circle. Sitting, focusing on breathing gently and then slowly lying down on their backs. They can do this one after the other, everyone 'letting go'.

Balancing the Energy
We have probably all experienced the sort of class that feels like it's running away with you. If you don't hang on you'll fall off with a crash. And conversely the sort of class which feels too 'good', boring and slow. Accept these uncomfortable feelings as a necessary part of 'getting in tune' with your class. Also, think what *you* need to do for yourself, perhaps stretch yourself out or do some faster energetic stuff. Begin to notice and trust how *your* body is feeling and you will be sensitive to the feelings of others. Use the breathing exercises for yourself too.

Gradually, a nice ebb and flow of ideas will begin as you all relax and enjoy striving and thinking and creating and having some fun together. Take time to notice the children's *response* to ideas. Talk about that to them. (*See also 4.*)

23 Aspects of the Lesson

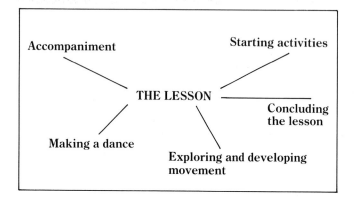

Starting Activities

24 Beginning the Lesson

Teachers sometimes worry about children feeling self-conscious and perhaps they themselves feel self-conscious too, but this usually goes as soon as the childen become interested and involved in the movement. It is a good idea to sit and talk a little first. For example:

> 'What we will do is . . .'
> 'Can you think of some ways to warm up?'
> 'Do you remember . . . ?', etc.

It is useful to have a standard way of beginning the lessons, the children perhaps sitting near the teacher initially to ensure involvement before moving out into the space. The movement can graduate from *sitting* to moving *in place* to *travelling* about the room.

Begin very simply with unison movements, all sitting or standing near or in a circle so that nobody feels isolated or obtrusive. Moving in unison often produces a stronger sense of involvement. It focuses the energy and the discipline involved shapes the children's response and awareness.

Use specific exercises to encourage body skill and awareness, or listening and concentrating. Stress large movements to offset the cramped movement which many children have. Stress the spine bending and stretching particularly. And use imagery from the book or colourful language to communicate the idea. Use repetition and clear accompaniment. Repetition heightens involvement and can be used to find out *more* about the movement. More detail will then emerge.

25 Relaxation

Contrast different types of movements, otherwise children become tense. Practise 'letting go', flopping out on the floor or, from standing, letting the head and upper body hang down, keeping the feet straight. Encourage movements that flow easily from one to another. Rhythmic ability is blocked by tension.

Use these exercises to encourage children to feel their weight. They may be used in other parts of the lesson as well.

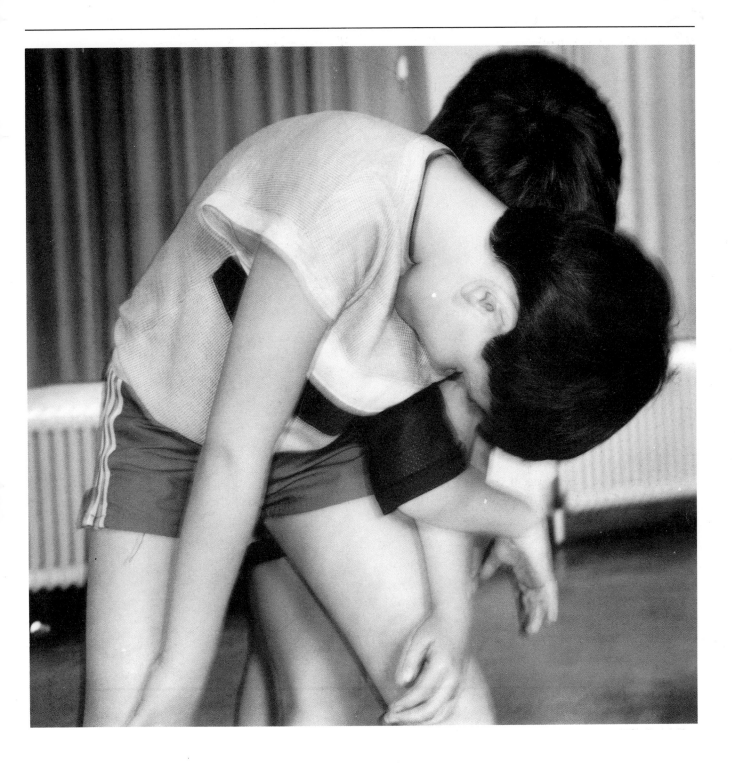

Hang down from standing with feet straight and a little apart. Make sure your *knees* stay apart. Feel your heavy head pulling your upper body *down*. Let a partner gently trace all the way down your spine from the base to the head. Imagine a waterfall running down your spine and off your head.

Lie on your back and *breathe* and feel all the parts of your body that are touching the floor. Let go of yourself. If your teacher picks up your arm or leg, it should feel heavy and floppy.

Roll with your knees pulled up into another lying down position as if you are melting into the floor. Roll and stop, slowly, gently. Let your head relax into the floor too. Roll up into a sitting position and let your shoulders, head and arms hang down.

26 Self Massage

Use rubbing and pressing movements to warm and energise the legs, ankles and feet, to feel around shoulder and elbow joints, to press into and release the muscles at the base of the neck, etc. Self massage is a good way to begin or end a lesson, heightening as it does the awareness of the body.

27 Breathing

Breathing and energy are interconnected. Many children hold their breath, creating physical tension, particularly when they are 'trying' hard.

Encourage childen to listen to their breathing, to notice which parts of their bodies are involved in their breathing. Suggest that they lie on their backs and feel how they can breathe right down into their stomachs rather than high up in their chests. Use images like:

imagine breathing into all of yourself. Imagine the breath going down your spine into your legs, through your back, along your arms, into your fingers, etc. Imagine the breath is like a wave washing all through you. Imagine the air you breathe in is full of energy. It gives energy to . . .

For a *short* space of time children enjoy focusing on connecting *moving* and *breathing*.

From sitting — rounding forwards and downwards as they exhale — emptying out the air.
From any position stretching out away from the centre of the body as they exhale — 'blowing out' the stretch.
Jumping, a pouncing jump, towards the floor as they exhale.
Leaping upward as they exhale. Spiralling down to the floor with a long sigh.

The in-breath becomes the preparation to move. In the exercises, notice movements of connection between breathing and moving. Breathing and moving merge together, The movement feels more alive. (*See also* **7**.)

The following lists can be used as a basis for ideas. Select two or three ideas to suit the age and experience of the children. Use Contrasts (**15-18**) for further ideas.

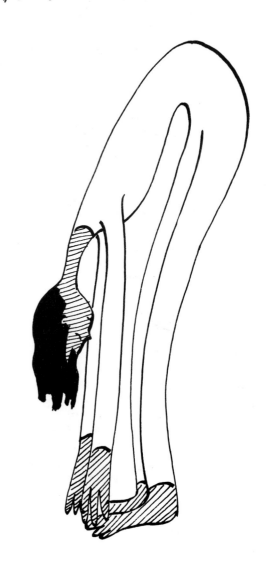

Hang down and let go

28 Lying, Sitting or Kneeling Movements

Make sequences.

Back	Sit straight with long back; imagine the head floating up into space; slowly drop the head down towards the feet curving forwards and breathing out. Sit up again and feel your straight spine. Arch your back and look up; twist and look behind but keep the spine long.
Shoulders	Lift them and drop them; circle them and shrug them; loosen and move them.
Back of the legs and back	Stretch your legs and your back by holding your ankles and walking your feet forward until your head goes to your knees and your legs are *straight*.
Arms	Stretch high overhead, then twist and turn the arms. Involve the back and the shoulders by stretching the elbows up, down, around in the space about you.
On hands and knees	Wriggle, arch and stretch your back. Bring your spine ALIVE like a snake. Sit back on to your heels and stretch forward, like a cat. Breathe deeply.
Sitting hand movement	Open them wide; grip them tight; rotate the wrists.

Spine Wriggling

Finger tips on the floor;
wrists on the floor;
palms on the floor;
shake them all about.

Press the palms together and relax
   (repeat);
(feel this movement in the whole body).

Head	Drop and lift from side to side (floppy head); circle and lift.
Lying down on the back	Stretch out like a starfish. Moving from the centre of your body, curl up tight on your side. Then slowly roll on to your back again. Repeat on the other side.
On your side	Arms straight overhead. Legs straight and together. Arch back, curve backwards like a *banana* or a crescent moon. Then curl up on your side with your knees to your chin like a ball. Arch and curl and roll around. Get your spine and the centre of your body MOVING.

Lie down. Gently swing your feet over your head then rock up to sitting. Do BACK ROLLS to stretch your spine.

Find some good ways to come from lying down to sitting to standing. Then SLIDE your way down again. Turn yourself UPSIDE DOWN. Shoot your toes into the air in a shoulder stand. Roll down.

Copy	The teacher's body part; copy hand, elbow, hand movements (this is a good attention-catcher).
Move slowly	Body-part movement. The children choose: elbow moves; head moves. Then slow, big arm movements. Hold the shape you are in. Remember it. Slowly stand to find a space in the room. Sit in the remembered shape.
Counting up and down	Stand slowly over six beats and sit down over six beats (or four or two etc). Stand over two beats; sit down over two beats; stand on ONE beat.

(Any of these movements could be developed into whole body movements.)

Cat Stretch

29 Moving 'in Place'

Two contrasting sounds	On a tambourine; bounce hands or feet; shake hands or feet.
Tight roll into	Roll, curled up tight, then stretch out into a balance on a body part. Stress the spine stretching or arching. Pick out one child's action and all practise that one.
Body swings (like swingboats)	From up to down and side to side and forwards and back. Stretch high to the side then drop down deep and up the other side. Bend the knees, make the swing big and continuous.
Standing, stretching and bending the spine (like elastic)	From standing, stretch high with right hand then left. Stretch, stretch and drop down. Stretch over to the side, forwards and backwards, downwards and upwards.
Clap and stretch	Clap high overhead; clap low near the ground; clap high again; lunge clap forward (front leg bent, back leg stretched). Make a clap rhythm.
Stretching the legs	In crouch position place the hands on the floor, straighten the legs and then bend them back into crouch. Lie on the floor on the back, legs straight and together. Bend one leg and stretch it up, like a signpost. Bend it and place it on the ground again. Repeat with the other leg. Make variations of this idea.
Hanging down	Stretch high, then relax down through the fingertips, elbows, head, back, knees and up again. Use different speeds.
Shaking sequences	Shake the right foot as you hop; shake the left foot as you hop. Eight hops each side. Then four hops. Then two and one.

Rocking	From foot to foot (*feeling* the foot); from side to side or forward and back, with a straight body.
Springing feet	Stand with feet together, then spring softly from foot to foot on the spot, bending the feet as much as possible.
Arrow legs and arms	Pull the foot into the knee and shoot it out into space; bend the arm and hand close to the body and shoot the fingers into the air; make fast rhythms; use all directions.
Arm movements (These can go with the above jumps.)	Swinging with opening and closing movement — big circles 'lassoing' — big circles shooting out.
Jumping (header jumps)	Jump with feet together, head high.
(frog or star)	Jump from crouch position to wide in the air; knee jumps with knees high; turning jumps; jumps off two feet into one and vice versa (as in hopscotch).

30 Travelling About the Room

Running and stopping	Out of a space and back to it. Run and stop. Press the back high, hands and feet on the floor (like a bridge). Run and stop. Lie down. Press toes in the air.
Flying and balancing	Run, arms outstretched. Balance on one leg. Lift the other one high.
Gallop steps	Bent knees or stretched legs. Go in different directions, with right or left side leading, to a rhythm.
Skipping	as above.
Leaping along	landing on one or two feet.
Crawling	by *stretching* the hands forward alternately along the ground, pulling knees right up to the body.
Sliding	along, pulling the body forwards with the arms, or sliding on the back or side.
Wriggling	along fast.

Walking (centipede)	on all fours with *straight* legs and arms, bringing the feet close to the hands. This can also be done by walking the feet up to the hands and then walking the hands forward. Perhaps let the hips rest on the floor and arch back to finish.
Stepping patterns	Forwards; backwards; sideways; sequences; (lifting the knees or with straight legs, pointing the feet or with springing and hopping added).

These starting activities, sitting or kneeling movements, moving in place or travelling about the room, constitute a body-training session at the beginning of the lesson. Many of the movements might arise during creative work, but the stress here is on enlivening and disciplining the body. Each movement or sequence is repeated exactly several times. Vary 'soft' movements and energetic ones. Use plenty of 'relaxation' movements and link 'exhale' breathing to the movement.

Starting activities may not necessarily lead directly to the main part of the lesson. A contrast may sometimes be better. Focus on contrasts in each lesson.

Remember to choose a few contrasting starting activities at the beginning of each lesson. Many starting activities *could* grow into a dance if they were used *creatively* in the middle part of the lesson.

31 Using the Space

Children need practice in finding a space, in distinguishing between moving in or about the room and in spacing themselves in relationship to other children. Link this with any of the above ideas.

Practise:

finding a space and returning to the teacher;
travelling out of your space and *back* to it again, as if the space is 'home';
travelling from *one* space to *another* with skipping, galloping, creeping, etc. With young or insecure children it is sometimes helpful if the children *follow* the teacher initially into new spaces using a simple travelling and stopping phrase;
exploring the space around the body. Try to use up all the space around.

32 Accompaniment in Starting Activities

Use word rhythms and voice rhythms to accompany the movement. But also allow silence for the children's own rhythmic response. Vary this with the use of music and simple percussion.

Use VOICE — PERCUSSION — SILENCE — MUSIC. One piece of music can often be used for several starting activities. Music helps to involve the body and can be interspersed with the teacher's percussion playing. However, the teacher may well find it easier not to use music at this stage when her whole attention needs to be on the children. A tambour rhythm is often more immediate and effective.

Folk and ethnic music is useful for skipping, hopping or galloping step combinations.

These steps might be a basis for practice in co-ordinating actions and to 'get the body going'. The teacher must decide where in the lesson music is most needed. Be aware of the restrictions imposed on dance by a repetitive beat and perpetual syncopation. (*See also* **8-9**.)

33 Diagram of Starting Activities

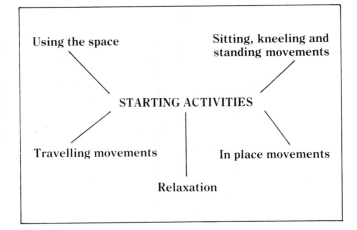

Exploring and Developing Movement

34 Development

This can be seen in terms of *depth* and *variety* in both skill and creativity. (*See* **10,14**.) It involves deepening the awareness of the action, improving the child's movement response and finding other ways or variations of the movement, so that it becomes both more vivid and more varied.

This movement experience might be compared to a language experience where the child is encouraged to expand his awareness in language: 'It's an apple. It's red. It's got a rough skin. There's a hole in it. It's all crinkly on one side.' He is encouraged to 'look' more closely at an object. He is encouraged to 'feel' more vividly in movement.

Encourage listening and moving, watching and moving, thinking and moving, in order to concentrate attention on the body. No creative dance can take place without this focusing of attention and subsequent enlivening of the body.

35 Improvement

It is very important to improve the performance of the child's response. This can be done in a sensitive way using praise and encouragement. Too often children are asked to 'explore' in a multitude of ways and never given time to become really involved in movement. The improvement might be movements suggested by the teacher or ones initiated by the child, and include for example:

improving the rhythm and flow of the movement
improving the use of the body parts in the action
improving the quality of the movement. (*See* **10**.)

Above all, stress that the whole body must be involved in the movement.

'Can you move your feet more quickly?'
'Are your fingers moving in the air very lightly?'
'Make your head float gently too.'
'Stretch your feet.'
'Make it clear what shape you are in the air.'

Accompaniment and improvement
The quality of the action and the performance of it can be greatly enhanced by the children sitting and *listening* to the accompaniment. For example:
  (a) Indian bells accompaniment
     'Can you move as softly as this? Move carefully.'
  (b) A tambour accompaniment
     'Listen to the loud accent in the rhythm. Can you make your leap fit in?'

36 Variations

From any action word idea, any number of movements may grow.

Walking variations
Walking can be performed forwards, backwards, sideways, very fast or slowly, smoothly or erratically. Walking can be by oneself or with a partner. We usually walk on our whole foot but we can also walk on different parts of the foot and on different parts of the body: on the heels, knees and hands etc.

All these ways give different expressions in movement. Remember that creativity in movement is not a cataloguing of possibilities but the *growth* of movement ideas, the growth of one movement to the next. The child's variation is his own way of interpreting an idea. This does not mean that the movement has never been done before, but that his particular movement is personal to him. Creativity is possible within very small limits.

There is a moment when absorption in the movement and in the limitation provided produce a fusion between the given ideas and the child's unique response to them. He begins to create *his* sequence, to feel his own rhythm. His whole body will be involved. There will be an absorption in his face and a tenacity about his practice. Such absorption does not come immediately, but the right conditions will help it to grow.

37 Questions and Tasks

Teachers can develop variations by asking questions on the movement and giving tasks. Questions offer choices and stimulate individual response. Tasks will encourage improving the movement and give examples of ways of moving. Remember that questions and tasks can be about:

> the body
> the quality of movement
> the space
> the relationship.

'Walking' was cited as an easily understood action. Any other action can be varied in similar ways.

Examples of questions and tasks

What?	'Show me a "header" jump with the head going really high. What other part could go high?' 'What do your arms do as you turn?' 'What do you look like (shape) as you stop?'
How?	'Crawl really slowly stretching your arms and legs.' 'Are you falling slowly or quickly?' 'Can you show me three strong arm positions?'
Where?	'Where are your hands as you stop?' 'Show me dodging forward and stop.' 'Which way (direction) are you going to skip?'

Some more general questions:

'How could you make the movement clearer?'
'How would it fit with a partner?'
'What would happen if you tried it this way?'

Give *time* for response.

Questions and tasks can be varied endlessly. Some tasks offer more freedom of choice than others. For example, 'Listen to the rhythm. Show me what your feet do — what can your feet do to this rhythm?' or, 'Try three stamps and a leap. Ready . . . !' Both tasks have plenty of scope for creativity.

Try to keep a balance between improving and varying. Never over-develop one movement idea beyond the concentration and interest of the children.

38 Observation

It is partly through her knowledge of movement, and partly through her observation of the child's response that the teacher's facility for developing movement ideas increases. Observation can be the starting point for variation or improvement. For example, if the arms are uninvolved, the teacher and children can think what the arms could be doing, and practise the ideas.

The movements of one child can be noted and the ideas shared with the rest of the class, who can all practise them, with a common rhythm following the teacher's accompaniment. This is especially helpful for a child with poor movement ability. But do not make children demonstrate their work individually or in very small groups unless you are sure of their confidence to do so.

Try to select *movement* ideas from observing the children. This is more encouraging to creativity than merely noting that a particular child's movement is 'good'. Encourage phrases and rhythms that come from the children. Encourage them to be aware of their own movements. There comes a time when children are ready to repeat and select in some depth, but beware of forcing this at too early a stage.

Give opportunities for the children to watch and observe each other.

It is fun to 'pick up' on something that you see and copy it, or think of an opposite response.

This 'kinesthetic observation' is as important as talking about what you see.

Through observation children gradually develop a critical appreciation of dance.

The Dance

39 Selecting Ideas

From the movement experiences of the lesson, some are selected, a beginning is chosen and an end is created. (*See* **21**.) A dance is made, however impromptu. The degree of selection and skill will vary according to the age and ability of the children. In the example lesson (***Part 3***), indications are given of the sort of dance which might arise from the initial actions. There are no rules about this. The dance is the result of the interaction between the movement, the teacher and the children.

The essence of the dance can usually be remembered and repeated another time. The dance might be developed or added to. Older children may recapture exact phrases, others will remake and re-explore. Very young children do not seem to need this end-product in the same way. What matters to them is the flow and delight of the movement experience.

In essence there are as many forms of dance as there are imaginations to make them, but a few practical frameworks can be useful.

40 A Teacher and Class Dance

Here the choice can be between dancing near to the teacher or away from her, back to her, around her.

For example, the children dance near the teacher, bouncing and clapping. She sends them off into space where they dance on their 'own spot'. She brings them back to her and the dance ends with the shared action of ·turning, arriving low and then remaining still.

Being 'near or far' from the teacher and 'doing the same or different' is a useful format for an infant dance, where the children need the security of the teacher's proximity. The children are guided by the teacher and fun can be had in the sending away and the coming back.

41 A Partner Dance

In the early stages this can be simply dancing *near* the partner. Suggest 'fitting in' together, beginning and ending together. Body shapes can clarify the beginning and ending.

Other variations involve: doing the same *action* or different; *where* they go — up, down, towards, away or following their partner; *when* they move — at the same time or one after the other.

Gradually encourage sensitivity to touch and work in contact.

'Stay with your partner and then move on your own. Then come back again.' This is a nice framework for moving in and out of contact.

Encourage them to watch each other, to make their movement relationship clear. These suggestions can be practised separately. Other ways will arise from a variety of dance situations. All kinds of expressions arise (copying, agreeing, sharing, friendly, antagonistic) when dancing *with* someone.

42 A Small Group Dance

Small groups of children can work in a similar way. Working within a group is demanding both in movement control and socially. The action content must be *simpler* than when working individually. Young or inexperienced children will tend to lose movement quality if group work is demanded of them too early.

Groups might intermingle using similar actions; dance towards, away or round the centre; change the shape of the group by coming close together, making a file or a circle; move together with other groups or one after the other. It's fun if, without talking and just through quick observation, one group 'picks up' the movement of another.

43 An Individual Dance

This can be made at all levels of ability. The length and complexity will vary accordingly. The individual dance can be a short sequence or a more extended composition where a degree of repetition and selection has resulted in a fixed form. The dance is the individual's. He knows how it begins, grows and ends.

44 A Follow-my-leader Dance

In pairs or small groups, the dance may be built on a particular formation. The file might use an action which was particularly enjoyed in the lesson. Quick observation and response are needed. The leader must be sensitive to the children following.

The leader can be changed so that each child has a chance to lead and respond. Small group dances, where a variety of movement is going on, often lead very well into a unison file dance.

45 A Circle Dance

A circle dance form can be used during the lesson tasks and in the making of a dance. A circle is a secure framework for movement. Teach the children to make a circle quickly, to move in the circle skilfully.

The children can dance around in a circle; into the middle and out; across the middle to change place; making the circle grow larger, smaller.

Circles can respond to the movement of the person in the centre, copying or responding to the steps, arm gestures, body shape, etc. of the one in the middle of the circle.

46 A Half-the-class Dance

A circle formation is a useful form for:

half the class moving around (X)
half the class sitting in the centre (O)
half the class dancing (X)
half the class making accompaniment sounds (O).

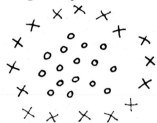

In addition, half the class may sit by the teacher and half the class dance:

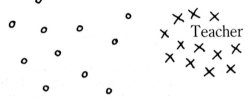

or, half the children stand 'statues' while the other half travel among them.

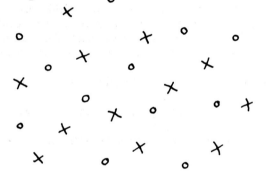

47 Dance Forms in Composition

Any combinations of these ideas may fall into particular dance forms. The form or shape of the dance will often emerge during the working process. It is useful to keep a few in mind while realizing that there is an immense variety of forms and a lack of theoretical knowledge need not inhibit using an intuitive awareness of form.

Think of each movement idea or section as being indicated by a letter of the alphabet so that, for example, a dance may consist of part A followed by part B and then a repeat of part A. Some element of A might be changed in the repetition, for instance, 'Do altogether in unison what you originally did with your partner.'
So the dance might have a pattern of

A B A
A B A C A B A A
A B C B A
A A B B   or *one* idea might be varied endlessly.

Accompaniment

The importance of accompaniment in the lesson has already been stressed in **8** and **9**. Any examples and tasks must be clearly accompanied.

48 Unaccompanied Movement

When the children are asked to explore and find their own variations, give them a chance to do so, without accompaniment. During this practice time, which may be very short, the teacher moves about among the children, encouraging them and giving occasional accompaniment help to individuals or groups. It is useful to give a time span for this practice. For example, 'When I tap on the tambour, you begin. When I tap again, you stop.' In this way they learn to develop their own movement rhythms.

49 Music as Accompaniment

Music can be a wonderful stimulus for enlivening the body (*see 32*), although other forms of accompaniment are often simpler and evoke more immediate responses.

Choose music with care. Remember that the dance is *using* the music and it is the development of the movement that must be stressed. Music can help the development of the movement idea, but music alone will not *provide* the movement ideas.

Choose pieces which are rhythmically simple or have a very clear mood content. Symphonic movements or heavily orchestrated pieces where the phrasing is uneven are not usually suitable for children's dance. Remember to use a variety of music differing in tempo, rhythm and volume. Seek out music and the sound of instruments from different cultures to broaden and enrich the dance work, for example, tabla music, African drumming, steel band, South American rhythm and melody, Japanese flute, etc.

Children can make phrases or movement *over* the music. They do not have to follow a rhythm slavishly. Music can run parallel to the dance and sometimes music and dance can intermingle.

Music can form a background for action, the movement relating to the mood and occasional accents in the music. For example, a group of children made a dance about strangely shaped, slow-moving creatures on the moon. Electronic music was later played as a background to the movement. Sudden accents in movement were related to sudden accents in the music. Here 'how' the children moved, i.e. slowly and carefully, was echoed by the slow, strange quality of the music, but the rhythm of the movement came from the nature of the actions.

50 Music and the Lesson Plan

The same piece of music can often be used for one of the starting activities as well as the dance. Percussion and voice might be used in the development part of the lesson as in *Skipping Dance 172*. Alternatively, music may be played at the end of the lesson to link with ideas experienced during the lesson (as in *Procession 171* and *Action Dance 167*.)

A list of suitable music may be found in the *Appendix*.

The short pieces can be used with starting activities and the lessons.

Encourage the children to listen, to notice the phrasing. Some may have a strong rhythmic sense and naturally dance in time, but it is equally important for them to sense the spirit of the music and use those same qualities in the movement. (*See 32*.)

51 Self-accompaniment with Voice Sounds

Here the children themselves make sound and movement together. If children make sounds as they move, the rhythm and quality of the movement are strengthened.

Introduce the idea gradually. Suggest that the children use voice accompaniment in a tiny part of the lesson. Always link making a sound to making a movement. Sound and movement can be clarified simultaneously. Encourage sensitive interaction between sound and movement by such tasks as:

'Make your sound fit your action.'
'Make your sound stop when you do.'
'Sit on the floor and imagine your sound and your movement.'

Voice sounds may be linked with the actions of: growing slowly, leaping, turning, jerking, falling.

52 Conducting Voice Sounds

The children sit in front of the teacher. The teacher 'conducts' sounds. The teacher performs the action with her hands. She makes her hands move and stop. The children make a sound for the action, for example, humming or explosive syllables. The sound must mirror the action and stop when the hands stop.

The teacher's hands open and close slowly, rise high and sink with a wave-like motion, shoot upwards, drop down.

The children respond with their own individual sounds. A mixture of sounds is often much more powerful than a unison one.

The sounds could be tape-recorded. (*See 175*.) In these ways the teacher guides sound and movement-making. Children can move as they make sounds or observe and accompany each other.

53 Accompanying a Partner

This idea can be developed into partner work. One child moves while his partner accompanies him. This should be done with a very simple action phrase (use the above examples), making sure once again that there is a beginning and an ending to the movement. Or the whole class can accompany, with voice sounds, one child moving in the centre of the circle, so the mover is in effect 'conducting' the sounds through his own movements. Make sounds when the one in the centre moves and be silent whenever he or she pauses.

In the same way, voice sound can be added to, or grow with, a group composition.

Sounds used as accompaniment might equally well stimulate movement and vice versa.

For simplicity's sake, sound as a stimulus is included in Part 2.

Part 2

Ideas for Dance

54 Relating Movement to the World Around Us

As indicated in Part 1 the body and its movement, its action and rhythm can be the content of a dance. The movement can equally well be related to feelings, experiences and activities in the world around us. Classroom activities, projects, writing or artwork may give rise to movement ideas. There is a natural interplay between movement and ideas. Movement relates fundamentally to so many activities that it can be a unifying element in education.

55 Encouraging Children's Observation

Children can be encouraged to see, feel and hear movement in the world around them — to see the shapes of buildings, the flight of a bird, to feel the softness of fur or watch the flurrying movement of leaves caught in the wind. All these can be experienced as movement sensations and the child's sensitivity and response to everything around him developed.

56 Evaluating the Idea

The teacher must evaluate the idea. Is it one which suggests a variety of action ideas? Do the latter contain contrast? Can they be developed? If the stress is on movement development, the inducement is a *starting point* which can be referred back to, but does not have to dominate and perhaps limit the movement ideas. The stimulus should not be slavishly copied but used as fertile ground for the *selection* ideas. Above all the stimulus should relate to the *child's experience*.

Try using different stimuli and approaches to movement with children. Compare their responses in different situations. Remember that it is the *movement content* of the lesson which must capture the attention and excite the response.

Some children respond far more readily to *tactile* or *visual* stimuli where they do not have to make the mental association of image to movement. Use the senses — looking, listening and touching — as much as possible.

57 Imagery to Reinforce Movement

Imagery can enrich a movement experience by adding an imaginative framework to a movement idea. Use imagery incidentally throughout the lesson, so that movement is communicated more clearly through phrases such as 'As if you were walking on eggshells', 'lasso arms' or, 'snake-like movement'.

Using colourful language to help broaden movement sensation and understanding, the teacher can find images relevant to the movement and experience of her class. Adults have a far larger and more sophisticated store of images than children, whose different cultures and background must also be considered.

In the above example, imagery is used to *reinforce* movement ideas. Many such images will occur to the teacher on the spur of the moment. Imagery can also suggest or stimulate movement. (*See also* **7**.)

58 Imagery as a Stimulus

Here the image is used as a starting point for a variety of movement ideas. Obviously anything can be imagined. Generally speaking, the older the child, the more imagery *can* be used to provoke a quick movement response. There is little point in using images unless the child understands and is excited by them. Use images that arise from the children.

Allow time to experience the image. For example, children can lie down or sit with their eyes closed . . .

'Imagine you are . . . '
'What does it feel like . . . ?'
'How are you going to move?'

Many of the ideas in this book can be dwelt on in this way. Then select action words from the image as movement starting points. (*See* **170**.) Decide whether the image alone is a sufficient stimulus or whether it needs reinforcing with pictures, objects or music, etc.

59 Movement to Imagery

While it is stimulating to take an image as a movement stimulus, it is also worthwhile to work the other way round — for *movement* to suggest ideas to the children. This encourages individual associations of movement to images, and often results in very original ideas. (*See* **169** and **220**.) Even if the teacher *has* decided on using a particular image, it is often a good idea to explore the movement *before* mentioning the image. For example, a lesson on witches might be more effective if lots of witch-like movements were explored and *then* the children were asked to connect the idea of 'witch' to the movement, and make their own dances. (*See* **192**.)

Any of the images in the lessons in Part 3 could be used earlier or later in the lesson.

Note too that a particular basic movement might have any number of movement associations. For example, twisting **slowly might relate to the movement of a cat, of agony, smoke, etc.**

stretch

stop

fall

push

jump

Flash Cards

60 'Moving Words'

Flash cards of action words have proved a good movement stimulus. They capture attention and provoke an immediate movement response. Obviously the words must relate to the child's experience both in movement and reading. The development of language and movement skills can be closely linked, and the use of flash cards can reinforce both these skills.

Write the 'moving words' on large, brightly-coloured cards. Hold a card up. Ask the children to, 'Dance the word. Don't tell me. Show me!' and then quickly provide a simple rhythmic accompaniment to keep the movement going and improve the quality of the movement. Many of the lessons could include the use of flash cards.

61 Placement of Cards

The words might equally well be written on a *blackboard* or on a large sheet of *paper*. Then the action word can be *pointed* at, rather than held up.

If the children are organized to dance group by group, flash cards can be placed on the floor. Children dance beside the word and then move on to another. Encourage them to use as many ideas as possible, to make a dance moving around the word. One group of children actually carried words as they moved and kept on re-arranging them in difficult formations.

Think of other ways of using cards. Use ideas involving guessing, choosing, communicating, etc. In the classroom, movement might well be an aid to understanding and enjoying language. In the dance lesson, language stimulates movement, and it is the full *enactment* and *rhythm* of the latter which is of paramount importance. It is the immediacy of words to movement that is enjoyed.

62 Word 'Messages'

(*See* the list of **Action words, 11**.) Flash cards can be held up as 'messages'.

Stretch   Flop

Spin

Children dance the message. They can take it in turns to hold up the message to the class. The emphasis must be on the many ways they 'say' their message in movement. Can they make the message interesting to watch?

Then groups can each be given a 'secret' message. Each group has to guess the other group's messages from their movement.

('Messages' can also be interpreted through movement with sounds.) (*See* **212**.)

63 Words as Patterns

When the children are familiar with words, they enjoy patterns which 'look like' the action they represent.

Fall   Jump

64 Pair Words

Hold up two contrasting words and ask the children to link them together in movement — to 'join them up'. Seize upon the initial response and use accompaniment to enlarge and clarify the movement. Partner work could follow. Partners could dance in unison; for example, turning and jumping together, or one child might dance *jumping*, the other child dance *turning*.

Partner relationships, around each other, or beside each other, help the idea to grow into a partner dance.

65 A Stretch Card

A ten-foot-long 'stretch' card once delighted a group of children. They said the word as they stretched into elongated shapes. They also used the card as an object to stretch, stride along *beside* and stretch and jump over.

The idea grew into a *dance* when the action of rolling arose — because the card kept on rolling up! Stretching and rolling sequences developed. The card then became a cylindrical *enclosure*. Four children at a time crouched inside, stretched up, jumped out and stretched and rolled away.

Flash cards can be made by the teacher or the children and can arise from any classroom activity or topic. See the action word list (*11*) and combine this idea with any of the lessons.

66 Nouns and Adjectives

These can also be used on flash cards. Here the word or image has to be 'translated' into action.

Challenge the children to, 'Show me what you think of doing to this idea.' The word on the card is the stimulus for several action ideas. Unusual or colourful words arising from poems or topics might be explored in movement.

Pliable

Flight or Tunnel

EXPANSION

Movement Patterns

67 Drawing a Design

Many actions can be communicated through drawing simple designs. Use a sense of movement to produce design. For example, zig-zag, cover, circle, curve. This stimulus has been particularly effective where the children lack concentration and listening ability, or have language difficulties.

If the teacher draws the design with vivid colours on a large piece of paper *during* the dance lesson, the response is always very lively. The teacher draws, the children watch, then, without speaking, dance the design. Suggest to the children: 'Watch the movement design. What is it doing? Can you show me the movement?' Be ready to help with movement suggestions to encourage and develop the response. Draw bouncing, zig-zag, twisting or sliding patterns.

The size, quality and rhythm of the movement can be shown in the drawings. The movement communication is therefore very vivid, as in the following suggestions:

1 Draw a *large* twisting pattern.
2 Draw a large twisting pattern very *strongly*.
3 Draw it very *slowly* or *fast*.

Suggest the arms and hands lead the movement, then the foot or the elbow. Help them discover the changes of shape as the body moves.

Drawing a Design

68 Using Children's Designs

Making designs with paint or collage might well be a follow-up to a movement lesson and in turn stimulate dance ideas. Lesson *177* is an example of this. Words, movement and design are interrelated.

One teacher *combined* design making and dance within one lesson. A long strip of paper was placed down the centre of the room. The children each had their *drawing* space (kneeling by the paper) and their *moving* space. The method was to move and then draw, trying to use the same *quality*, i.e. light, strong, large, in the drawing as in the movement.

Coloured chalks and fat pens were used. Afterwards the design was worked on and a long vivid pattern produced. The pattern was then the stimulus for a subsequent lesson. Obviously careful selection of *movement* ideas is needed.

On another occasion children visited a gallery where they had the opportunity to paint and produce huge colourful designs, i.e. non-figurative paintings. These were subsequently used as starting points for movement and *sounds*. There was a moving group and a sound group using a combination of percussion and voice.

69 Design for an Overhead Projector

In a similar way, children have drawn simple designs for an overhead projector and their designs have been projected and used as a dance stimulus. Care must be taken that the patterns and designs are given due importance, and that they become colourful works in their own right, not mere representations of movement.

70 String Designs and other Materials

Using large pieces of coloured card, string designs can be made that relate to ideas of rising — sinking, stretching, curling, round and round, to movement.

Stick the string on in any large designs. This will encourage ideas for movement, groupings and floor patterns. Other materials — wool, fabric, sand, bits of plastic, etc. — can be incorporated into a design work.

Relating movement to pattern in this way will lead the children to a greater awareness of pattern in life around them. For some children, this method has an immediacy, a non-verbal or non-listening approach, which manages to involve them where other approaches have been less successful.

71 Design in the Environment

Patterns and shapes are all around in the natural and man-made environment. Relate the movement experience to the visual one by noticing patterns on trees, walls, car wheels, leaves, pavements, curtains, shells, radiators and clothes. This list can go on and on. There are also good slide collections about patterns and designs and sometimes the name of the source material can be used as the accompaniment to moving, for example:

pteropod — the name of a shell
Ferrari — for the circling movement design of a car wheel

Perhaps the most effective teaching method, after a vigorous warm-up, is (as with the objects or flash cards) to ask the children to *look* at the stimuli and then move immediately without talking, into a movement or a body shape. The moving in silence brings about a concentration on an idea, however slight. The children need to show their idea in *movement*, not words. Action words then help to clarify the response, for example, 'I liked that rolling along very small, then enlarging the movement into a sharp shape.' After this initial work the children will also respond readily to patterns in modern paintings. (*See 112, 175-7.*)

Objects

72 Moving Things

Things that move, or can be moved, are invaluable in quickly involving children and suggesting ways of moving. Words alone are often not enough. Children only need to *watch* intently and with that empathy very evident in children they will quickly respond in movement. Teachers who have classes with language problems find this approach useful. Language and movement can be extended simultaneously. Small, easily managed objects are most suitable.

73 A List of Things to Watch and Touch

Movement as the Keynote *7*, enlarges on the importance of touch.

Some of these can be handled so that sensitivity to their quality increases. For example, set up a 'touch table'; sit in a circle and slowly pass and feel different textured/shaped objects around the circle. Very often the shape of the object will suggest starting and ending positions. Remember that the movement can always be experienced in a part of the body as well as in whole body movements. For example, a fish movement can be expressed by hands darting and gliding in the space around the body, then the whole body gliding into a new space.

Many things do not 'do' anything, but action words can be linked with them. For example, a rock suggests pressing strongly into different shapes, rolling and balancing. (*See also 113.*)

Often the simplest things, like a piece of paper being blown along, can set off ideas.

Watch and Touch

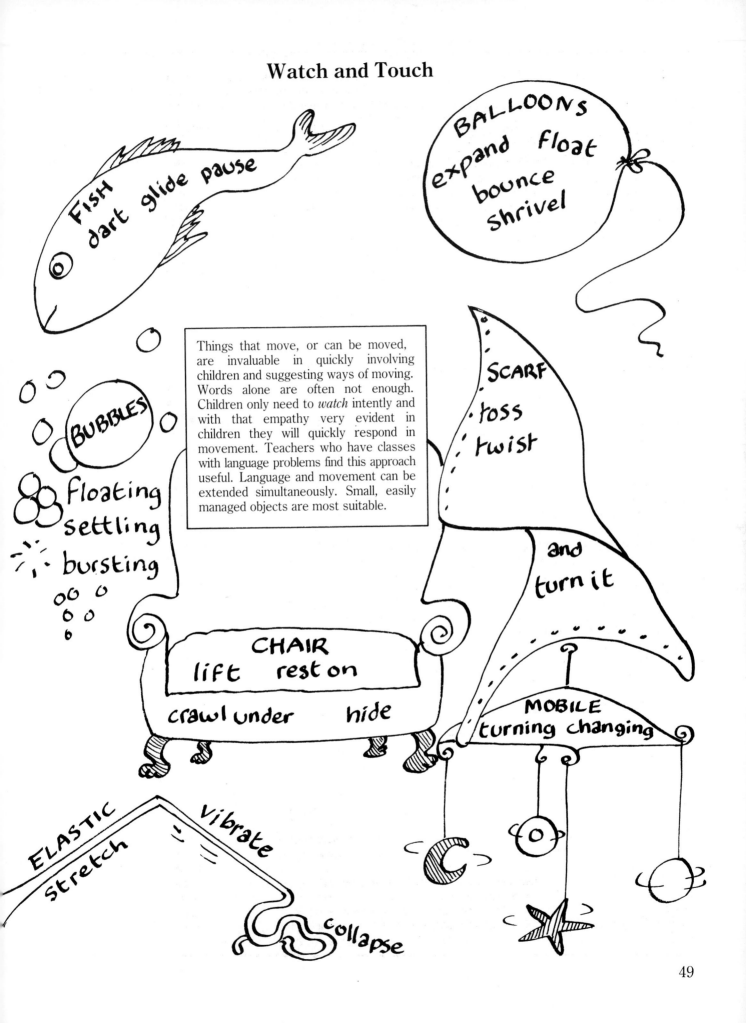

FISH dart glide pause

BALLOONS expand float bounce shrivel

BUBBLES floating settling bursting

SCARF
- toss
- twist

and turn it

Things that move, or can be moved, are invaluable in quickly involving children and suggesting ways of moving. Words alone are often not enough. Children only need to *watch* intently and with that empathy very evident in children they will quickly respond in movement. Teachers who have classes with language problems find this approach useful. Language and movement can be extended simultaneously. Small, easily managed objects are most suitable.

CHAIR lift rest on
crawl under hide

MOBILE turning changing

ELASTIC stretch vibrate collapse

74 Objects with Sounds

Sometimes the chosen object will make a sound as it moves, and then there is a double stimulus of suggested movement and a given phrase of sound. Elastic 'pings' back to size. Children can 'grow' to the sound of the teacher (or their partner) 'blowing them up'; a top has a humming sound. Appropriate voice sounds can be added to the movement by the teacher or the children. If making the sound seems only to distract the children instead of helping the movement quality, they probably are not ready to combine movement and sound. (*See* **51**.)

Dividing up the class
It is possible to divide the different movement elements of the object between the class. For example: balloon; half the pupils grow, balance and crumple; half float gently among them.

75 Small Toys

These have been most useful because of the simplicity of their movement: a soft floppy animal, rag doll, spinning top, small rocking horse, ball, cotton-reel snake. A variety of action words arise: flop, spin, rock, collapse, balance, jerk.

The teacher can ask, 'What does it do? (Make it move.) Can you do that?' and give the children a chance to answer in movement. Then the focus must be on the children's response and its development. There is little value in just copying exactly what the thing does.

Action words can help to define the movement. The actions can be practised singly, then in simple combinations, or the movement might be varied by practising the action with different body parts and different body shapes. (*See* **182** *and* **185**.)

When working with young children, real things that move are very stimulating. Nursery and infant school teachers have made their own — floppy dolls, beanbag frogs, a rag octopus, stocking snakes, paper-bag puppets, a crêpe-paper swisher, a spinning spiral, a shape mobile — and used them with great success as movement guides and stimuli. At dance times (and with very young children this is probably not a formal lesson) they can stimulate qualitative action and simple phrases of movement. (*See* **183**.)

Of course, all these toys could be imagined and the ideas used in a toyshop dance with a framework of: wake up, move, go back to sleep again. Children of all ages enjoy this idea.

But as a movement stimulus the real thing has invariably proved a stronger stimulus to experiencing basic actions and qualities of movement.

Older children enjoy working in small groups using the object as a focus deriving moving ideas from, for example, an alarm clock or a magnet or a mobile.

76 Snake

'What is he doing? Yes, curling up very tight and stretching out *very* long. You do that. Ready! And curl up tight, tight and stretch out, stretch out l - o - n - g. And curl up . . .', etc.

Make the snake (a stuffed stocking) do lots of other movements that will stretch and bend the children's bodies up into the air, along the ground, from kneeling, lying or standing.

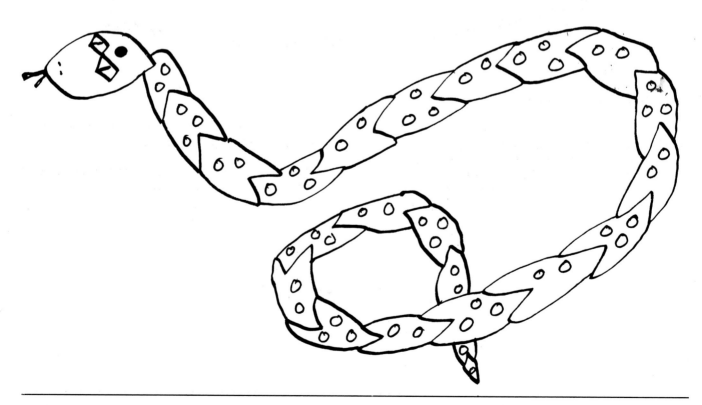

77 Paper-bag Puppet

The puppet can be a character — a soldier, marching and turning, or a clown, jumping and balancing.

The children do the movement with the puppet, or the puppet can be a king or magician character who tells the children what to do. This fantasy element encourages great involvement. Children have to listen to the puppet, watch the puppet. (*See* **Shaky King, 221**.)

Try making a collection of home-made movement stimuli. Give them names; make them personal.

78 Objects as Properties

Different actions will arise if the objects are used as properties while dancing. The quality of the property can be echoed in the body (*See 180* on dancing with a balloon.) Dancing with a light scarf, the teacher can ask 'Where does the scarf take you — up, down, around?'

With the idea of following the scarf, the whole body will stretch, bend and twist. Coloured crêpe paper, streamers, have been used similarly in a number of dances.

In the same way, dancing with small percussion instruments will stretch the body. Ideas for infants are Smarties tubes filled with something that rattles and secured with sticky tape. (*See Percussion Dance, 214.*)

Other objects to dance with are: chairs, cardboard boxes, cushions, dusters, newspapers, gloves, towels. For example, a cushion can be sat on, lifted high, pummelled, squeezed, stroked, jumped over.

A framework might be: 'Pick it up. Move with it. Put it down' to a clear timespan for movement. The objects can be danced with as things, or fantasy can change their nature and they become islands, enemies or magic properties.

Defining the movement
Any movement that arises can be clearly defined by thinking of the action phrase and what that consists of.

The teacher must decide whether the object is one to be *handled* and danced with, or *watched* — or a combination of the two. With less experienced children it is generally easier to try one object initially — a variety in one lesson will produce more ideas than it will be possible to develop.

The following lessons use objects: *178-189, 206* and *221.*

Dressing Up

79 Large Pieces of Cloth

Dressing up as a stimulus for dance can use the quality of the garment, how it affects the body's basic movement, rather than as a specific costume. Large pieces of cloth can become cloaks, camouflage or swirling skirts. (*See* **190**.) Ask 'How do you move in that costume?' Try to relate it to action words. Help the other children to watch, feel the movement, practise it to a voice rhythm. Little phrases of dance may be experienced in this way. The movement that resulted can be recaptured without necessarily wearing the costume and repeated many times so that it becomes part of the body vocabulary, such as 'Remember that really slow proud walk.' Clothes may suggest a character, for example, baggy trousers conjure up the idea of a clown.

80 Making Costumes

Fantasy costumes can be simply and quickly made, not necessarily with a specific character or costume in mind. Ideas will grow with the costume. Use a variety of materials; for example, strips of material, old stockings, newspaper, dustbin bags, paper plates, decorative bits and pieces to make head-dresses, body coverings and masks. 'Disposable' costumes can be made **on** the child. Play with the materials and see what effects you can create.

81 A Box of Costumes

The box is placed in the centre of the room. Half the class watches while the other half moves. One by one, each child walks to the box, takes a costume, puts it on, and then makes a statue in character in a space in the room.

At a given signal each child moves as his costume suggests, then stops, again in character. One by one the children replace the costumes and sit by the teacher. The accompaniment might be a drum-beat or quiet background music. Many older classes have performed this exercise with great absorption. It must be done with clear moving and stopping. Discussion about the movement follows. Define it in action words. Suggest how to make the movements larger and more rhythmic.

82 A List of Costumes

Costume wearing can be initiated in the classroom or by a few children as an introduction to the idea during a lesson. The movement can be realistic or fantastic.

Costumes can suggest movement ideas, or they can be used to make an existing dance more vivid. The following costumes and ideas have arisen in the past:

Shoes — a step rhythm. Step, step, lift (the knee), step, step, lift. 'Bouncing shoes' that will not stop.

Beret — head-shaking, nodding; the head takes you high, low, around, *follow* the head.

Skirt — turning, rising and sinking, and leg gestures, or try wearing it over the head.

Scarf — swirling, whirling, leaping dance if tied round the head; a creeping, pouncing bandit dance.

Any number of ideas will arise. Select and develop a few or help the children to do so, so that they have some *definite* movement idea to practise. Any such activity should not be attempted until the children have good control of going and stopping. (*See also* **138**.)

83 Fashion Show

Today movement and dance are often used in fashion shows. Dancers and designers collaborate.

Select a few exaggerated fashion items and use them as starting points for idiosyncratic ways of moving and body shapes. Or select certain movements embodied in a fashion show and create short sequences, repetitions, and unison movements.

Create individual or group pathways (cat walks) through the room. One particular group responded to the idea with the words, 'Exciting! Changeable! Explosive! My body's the wrong shape!' and used these words as a chant to accompany the movement.

84 Face Paints

Try 'dressing up' your own face. Use black and white or green or red. Change your face and change *how* you move. Who do you become? Let your face suggest movements to your arms and legs. Make a pattern of movements that takes you up and down in the space and shows clearly who you *are* with this new face!

People

85 Movement Characters

Different types of people have different movement characteristics. In our everyday language we talk about a 'pushy person' or a 'weak character'. People are defined as strong-minded, uptight, devious, woolly-minded, and these ideas can be interpreted by a variety of actions.

Practise the initial action type in sequences of action. For example, *a dithering person* — use small, light steps with frequent changes of direction, small, light hand and head movements, quick, light changes of position — this way, that way; *a strong person* — strong, striding steps, hand and arm gestures, emphatic jumps.

Make a phrase of movement which travels, then moves in place. Repeat it many times.

Alternatively, encourage the children to use contrasting qualitative movement and discover the sort of characters that emerge. Children could then develop one idea as 'their' character. This character could be given a name. Remember to guide the children to make a 'movement sentence' about their type of person.

Partner work — each character moving in turn, or *group work* — each group with a particular character (the lazy group, the happy group) might well follow.

The characters could be related to particular situations or people; for instance, school characters, family characters.

The more personal the ideas become, the more the children enjoy them. Any number of people can be depicted in movement by asking the children: 'How do they move?'; 'What actions do they use?'; 'What do they look like (body shape)?'

86 Clowns

Explore variations of walking and falling as the basic idea and make rhythmic sequences of movement, with a partner or the teacher. The emphasis is on a richness of funny ideas for walking and falling rather than mimetic clown actions. For example, walk on your heels with arms wide; turn with one leg high; fall over slowly; jump up again quickly.

Use a definite rhythm to practise the above phrases, then suggest the children make their own clown walks and falls. (*See* **Clowns 191.**)

87 The 'Mr Men' Books by Roger Hargreaves

These are a good source of ideas for young children. Select *one* main action word to 'describe' the character and use it in a variety of ways:

Mr Jelly

jelly walks
jelly hands
jelly head
jelly shapes
jelly jumps.

88 Ghosts

Use movement to a quiet humming and accompaniment: stretching *slowly* into wide shapes at different levels. Curling quickly and vice versa, then floating and turning slowly or quickly from one spot to another.

Groups of children can dance together in threes using different shapes and levels.

Ghosts appear and disappear from and into a variety of body positions. They intermingle. The dance accelerates into a fast, light, whirling dance. A sudden stop and the ghosts vanish. (The idea of *vanishing* provokes many movement ideas.)

This particular lesson was most successful when the movements were practised before the suggested imagery which arose originally from discussion about 'night time'. The children then had movement examples on which to base their expression of 'ghosts'. (*See also* **Fairytale Witches 192.**)

Moods and Emotions

89 Feelings

Feelings can be expressed through dance, but this is an area where the function of dance is often misunderstood.

Just to *feel* is not enough. It is the *movement expression* of the feeling that is important. Too often movement that expresses an emotion is unoriginal and unimaginative because the movement possibilities that arise from feeling have not been developed. The following examples relate movement to mood:

Anger could suggest punching, stamping, leaping and landing strongly. Work out 'anger' body designs with a partner.

Practice of single actions could develop into a sequence: two stamping steps forward, a high leap with punching arms, landing strongly. (*See* **193** *and* **217**.)

Sadness: slow walks to kneeling. sinking down slowly, rising strongly, rocking forwards and backwards or side to side at different speeds.

Happiness: light skipping, hands clapping, small, high accent jumps, meeting and parting and dancing around a partner.

Fear, laughter, patience or *impatience* can be similarly explored.

Make this work personal. Discuss 'our feelings' and how we show them through our movement. We can often tell when someone is tired, energetic, bored or sad. Have a quiet thinking/feeling time when everyone lies down for a few minutes. Then use suggestions from the children. Look at the News on television for real situations. Through dance we can identify with others in the world.

90 Mood Voice Sounds

Taped mood voice sounds have proved a good accompaniment to the above ideas. It is possible to make a collection of 'angry phrases' with the children. Make an angry word rhythm to accompany movement.

> No no no! . . .
> Go *away*! Go *away*! . . .
> I won't! I won't! . . .

Or everyone 'sounds' together, creating one minute of angry sounds.

91 'The Great Blueness'

This story, by Arnold Lobel, describes a town where everything is grey. The people are very tired of grey and ask the magician for help. He mixes a magic paint and everything is painted blue. Everyone is happy but then they become tired of blue. It makes them depressed. So then yellow paint is provided. Happiness . . . but then yellow hurts their eyes. Everywhere is painted red, but red makes them angry. In the end multicoloured paint is produced, using all the colours of the rainbow and everyone is happy.

Many movement ideas arise from this (compressed) story. It is so rich in possibilities that movement must be selected and planned carefully or the content will be superficially enacted. For example, have three groups. Each child in the group makes a short phase of movement for

1 feeling depressed or
2 hurt eyes or
3 anger

exaggerating the body shapes arising. Everyone dances a unison happy dance or painting dance between each of the above episodes.

Try making your own mood story based in a particular location.

Each group could begin and end with a 'picture', frozen, contrasting body positions which come to life and move, and then return to the picture.

Dance these faces and draw your own.

Animals

92 'How Do They Move?'

Children have a wonderful affinity with animals, real or fantastic, which provides a rich source of movement ideas. Perhaps use film or photographs as a starting point. Try to capture the *quality* of the animals' movement. The following examples indicate how movment phrases can be selected to give a dance-like rather than mimetic expression. Other animals can be similarly explored by asking, 'What do they do?' in action and 'How do they move?', and by selecting movement which brings about exciting contrasts of action, direction or rhythm. Emphasize the involvement of the whole body, not just definitive parts.

93 Wild Horse

A poem or a photograph of a *free wild horse* could initiate: a free-flow high gallop and pull up, gallop and swerve, head toss into body turn, heel-tossing jumps and sudden stops, sequences of the above.

The Wild, the Free

With flowing tail and flying mane
Wide nostrils never stretched by pain
Mouths bloodless to the bit or rein
And feet that iron never shod
And flanks unspurred by spur or rod
A thousand horse, the wild, the free
Like waves that flow o'er the sea.

Lord Byron

94 Dolphins

Dolphins leap and dive, twist in the air and dive and roll. Children can practise leaping with their heads, knees or chests high, slow-motion diving leading to rolling, stretching or pressing upwards. Half the class could leap while the other half dives.

95 Wild Animals

This topic requires careful selection of a few movement contrasts. Several characteristic movements might be worked on initially; then one or two favourites selected and explored in depth so that the children have a choice.

Monkeys — running on all fours, then running lightly on the feet. Four runs on all fours. Four runs on the feet. Sudden stops and starts.

Elephants — plodding and turning, stretching and bending the knees and ankles.

Seals — lying on the floor — arching back, stretched rolls, slithering. Develop one of the above sequences in pairs or groups by varying directions and adding actions; for example, elephant head-swings and heavy rolls.

Perhaps make a dance, contrasting the movement of wild animals with caged ones. Consider what you feel about this issue.

96 Primitive Animal Dances

Older children enjoy learning about primitive animal dances. Here the dancer becomes like the animal and imitates its movement qualities.

Certain characteristic phrases are repeated over and over again.

A deer

> ru u un, leap and swerve
> ru u un, leap and swerve.

Curt Sachs in *World History of the Dance* vividly describes the movement of several animal dances, where the selected movements are repeated and made rhythmic. He writes of primitive man's belief: 'To imitate animals means to win power over them'; or, 'To imitate them in their distinctive characteristics means taking and rendering useful their magic power.'

Make a list of animals and find two or three contrasting movements to characterize them. Make partner dances copying or following each other. Perhaps make masks to go with the idea. Set an atmosphere with a primitive drum beat.

97 Fantasy Creatures

The movement of imaginary creatures on another planet can be defined by the questions: 'How do they go?', 'How do they move?'

The following diagram indicates the phrases of action which may arise from such a stimulus. (*See also* **224**.)

Or, out of the marsh comes the SWAMP MONSTER with huge wet steps, shaking mud and water off himself. He leaps and rolls and makes menacing gestures to a slurping, bubbling accompaniment. Make some squashy noises to go with the movement.

Summary

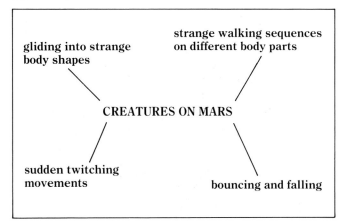

gliding into strange body shapes

strange walking sequences on different body parts

CREATURES ON MARS

sudden twitching movements

bouncing and falling

98 Animal Names as Stimuli

Children can invent names of strange animals. There are many examples of strange animal names in poetry books and stories, such as dinosaur names, for example, Diplodocus. These might stimulate ways of moving as in the 'Mars' example above, or the words might be used as rhythms to accompany strange movement. (*See* **Chants, 120** and Monsters, **196**.) (*See also* **194-195**.)

Cats

Cats are a wonderful source of qualitative movement and most children seem to have an immediate response to the sinuous stretches, rolls and sudden leaps that the ideas evoke and the 'sssst' sounds which can accompany them.

Slathery
Slithery
Hisser.
Don't miss her!
Run till you're dithery.
Hithery
Thithery
Pfitts! pfitts!
How she spits!
Spitch! Spatch!
Can't she scratch!

From *Cat* by Eleanor Farjeon in *That Way and This, Poetry for Creative Dance* (Chatto and Windus).

Nature

Nature is a rich source of movement ideas. Select action words which arise from the movement and shapes of the stimulus.

99 Water

Water suggests actions such as running and pausing, whirling and stopping, splashing up and rocking gently. These actions should be practised in phrases, co-ordinating different parts of the body and finding new movements. Then two actions might be linked together to form an action phrase.

> Splash *up* and *up* and *up* (getting different body parts high).
> Whirl STOP (opening the arms).
> Practise this.

One infant class enjoyed watching the *rocking* movement of water in a bowl, which produced a dream-like quality in the children's movement. (*See* **Water, 200.**)

As in many nature stimuli, the action of the water as above, or the action of the *people* in water, could be a starting point.

Movement of people in water — smoothly, slow motion —

> shoot up and glide down
> open and close arms and legs
> swirl and roll.

Imagine the water moving you.

'Start in crouch position. Shoot the fingers high and stretch. Come down gently with the palms leading'. (*See* ***Swimming pool, 225.***)

100 Disaster

In our everyday lives we frequently learn of natural disasters reminding us of our human frailty and the power of nature.

These events can be the basis of dance explorations concerned both with the movement of the natural event and with people's reactions to it. Through dance, contact can be made with *the reality of what is happening* to other people.

101 Volcano

Use illustrations or create vivid word pictures to focus on the idea. Use percussion accompaniment made by the children themselves (rumbling drum-beats, sudden accents) and perhaps tape-recorded. Discuss the movement ideas beforehand and have clear starting points in the lesson. Use the images of:

> lava — slowly rolling and spreading
> rocks — exploding upwards
> smoke — curling, swirling.

A dramatic effect is achieved if the children are free to decide when to explode upwards. Everyone has a slow turning preparation and then leaps upwards, all at different times. Small groups can explode one after the other. Body shapes in the air and on the ground can be clarified.

Think about the feelings of the people and the action of people running, dodging and stopping.

Choose two contrasting ideas to work on in the lesson and divide them between groups or partners.

102 Fire

Similarly fire can be explored by means of the words: writhe, twist and shoot.

Fire movement such as writhing, could begin in one part of the body and spread to other body parts, or begin with one child and spread to others.

Suggestions such as, 'Show me different parts of yourself shooting out like flames as I play the instrument', stimulate movement variety.

The dance could be done in a circle, the outer group writhing and twisting, the inner shooting out flames! One teacher brought in strips of red crêpe paper with which the children could whirl and move. 'The Fire of London' as a topic might relate very well to dance in this way.

103 Other Nature Suggestions

Other useful titles under nature include: Wind (*see 202*); River; Reflections; Rocks (*207*); Birds (*197*); Storm (*202*); Earthquake; Drought; Desert; Flowers (*111*); Oil wells.

When planning the idea it is helpful to jot down the movement possibilities and then select one or two. There is a danger with stimuli of trying to cover too many ideas so that no in-depth work is achieved. Older children will respond well to nature stimuli if these are put within very clearly defined frameworks, particularly where relationships are stressed.

104 Mirage

'Mirage' from the desert image initiated slow, light changes of level and shape within a group. A leader was chosen and the rest 'fitted in' with his movements, opening, closing, rising, sinking. Different group shapes emerged, melted away and reformed.

105 Class Walks and the Outdoors

Class walks can have a dual purpose of collecting natural objects (leaves, flowers, etc.) and observing movement. On returning, stick on or draw on a huge sheet of paper anything collected or seen. Write movement words near them. Very often the movement seen on the walk offers immediate stimulus for movement. For example, gulls circling and pausing or a piece of paper lifting and dropping in the wind.

The feel of the wind, the sun, the ground, walls, pavements — all these can be the basis for response in movement.
For example:

What does the wind do to me?
Find some movements against the wall (leaning on it, stretching along it, pushing off it).

Movement can take place outdoors and an outdoor dance made, or ideas can be taken inside and consolidated in a different environment. As well as exploring the physical qualities of living things, also consider a focus on today's environmental issues. (*See Ocean, pp.137-143.*)

Seasonal Events, Myths and Festivals

Use the seasonal events, stories and rituals from the different cultures and faiths within our society as a rich source of ideas for dance and as a way of communicating and sharing our cultural heritages. The use of masks, candles or lanterns, and the processions, symbolic offerings and special food rituals underlie many of the celebrations, and the 'story lines' are often similar from one culture to another.(*See 137-141.*)

106 Christmas

This is traditionally the time of the mime and the tableau. Integrate these with dance and music using simple combinations of action and step patterns arising from the qualities and rhythms of the character or situation. (*See 85.*)

For example, *The Crowd in Bethlehem.* People hurrying to find somewhere to sleep. Try:

1   hurrying and pausing (to a given drum-beat with lots of short phrases);
2   hurrying and pausing, changing direction and avoiding people;
3   beginning with hurrying and then slowing down to walking heavily;
4   sinking down to the ground slowly (tired), resting on one knee, or two, in different positions;
5   choosing when to hurry, when to pause, when to avoid, when to slow down, when to rest in a position.

The above example indicates the movement detail and repetition involved if the movement is to be clear and fully experienced. It is important to repeat each phrase many times so that rhythmic flow is developed.

Shepherds can move slowly from one position to another (lying, sitting, standing, kneeling) as they stretch, stamp their feet and swing their arms to keep warm, and look over the fields and into the sky, with a unison focus of 'look' as Gabriel appears.

Accompaniment Use percussion instruments for background sound, with tambours and woodblocks playing muted 'hurrying' rhythms for the crowd idea, or to accompany the rhythm of the movement. (Angels are exemplified in *203*; stars in *206*.)

Carols of different moods and rhythms have proved good accompaniments. Generally speaking, use the melodies and rhythms rather than the sense of the words to dance to.

A group of children suggested dancing to Christmas titles such as:

Candles — rising, sinking, turning in files or circles carrying candles.
Meeting friends — in groups of four; each child dances with each of the others; all four dance together.
Christmas presents — coming alive.
Mobiles — swaying.

107 Fireworks

Fireworks are a feature of many festivals; for example, Guy Fawkes Night and the Chinese New Year celebrations, when fireworks are set off as the Lion dance goes through the streets accompanied by drums and cymbals.

Use action ideas such as rockets — shooting up and sinking down; catherine wheels — whirling around or whirling parts of the body; crackerjacks — sudden small jumps and stops.

The rhythmic accompaniment is important. Give clear models and tasks, for example:
Crackerjacks

hop, hop, hop, *jump* (on to two feet)
hop, hop, hop, *jump.*

Remember that any action can be the basis of individual or group work.

Older children enjoyed making a rocket group shape using different levels and pointing a variety of body parts in one direction. They began swaying gently and built the sway into a crescendo which leapt them skywards. They sank gently down into different shapes at the end. This was practised many times over.

Use percussion accompaniment. (*See* **204**.)

108 Winter

Ideas for winter include 'What we see' and 'How do we move?'

1 *Ice*
freezing and melting (stretching into shapes and slowly 'melting')
ice groups forming, travelling and reforming.
Bring some ice into the lesson. Touch it and feel how cold it is, how slippy it is. React to these ideas of coldness and slipperiness in movement. Make some ice *word collages* as accompaniment.

icccccce . . .
cold shiver . . .

2 *Keeping warm*
stamping jumps alternating with swinging, beating arms. With jumping and swinging as an initial limitation all sorts of interesting movement combinations can arise.
Use lively music to accompany. Dress up in scarves, gloves, hats and use these as a source of movement ideas too. (*See* **205**.)

Outdoor Song

The more it
SNOWS — tiddely pom
The more it
GOES — tiddely pom
The more it
GOES — tiddely pom
On
Snowing

And nobody
KNOWS — tiddely pom
How cold my
TOES — tiddely pom
Are
Growing.

By A.A. Milne from *I Like This Poem* (Puffin edition).

Try tape recording this poem with percussion accompaniment at a *fast* pace. Use it for a foot warming dance of — steps-hops-steps and . . .

109 Halloween

Suggestions include:

Make phrases of movement from ideas of witches, night rides and magic. Dress up, make masks and use contrasts of slow/quick movements. (*See 192.*)

This topic is an exciting one. It is important to select a small number of movement starting points and *develop* them. Use voice chants or music to accompany. (*See 79.*)

Witches' den

A group of schools organized a witch afternoon. Classes from each school came together to make dance, sound effects and simple costumes. The hall was blacked out and decorated with witch paintings and strange mobiles. As he entered the den each child was stamped with the devil's mark (a pig's trotter dipped in ink). The children danced in groups to voice chants and percussion. (*See 192.*)

It is often a simple matter to enhance a dance with a few props which help to make the dance more vivid.

110 Harvest Time

The work action connected with harvest time can be linked in rhythmic phrases: throw, throw and rise (throwing seed); cut and cut and cut and rest (scything); stoop and lift and walk, walk, stoop and . . . (gathering).

Accompaniment might be a work song. Groups of children could dance different phrases. (*See 122 and 156* for ideas about 'call' and 'refrain'.)

Alternatively, select the ideas of the grow, sway and fall, a unison movement which might be performed simultaneously or one by one, to represent the idea of the growing and cutting down of the crop.

Once again the above example would only be used if it was connected with the children's own experience, such as through discussion of harvest time in different countries. Harvesting might equally well stimulate a dance about the movement of machinery!

111 Spring and Easter

The ideas embodied in the image of spring may be explored in a similar way. Ask the children for spring words (growing, opening, scattering) and make a spring dance.

Use perhaps a short extract from the beginnings of Debussy's 'Printemps' for opening, closing and turning flowers. Fade the music and play a gay rhythm on a tambourine for a happy spring dance. (*See 43.*)

A spring project could be combined with an *Easter egg dance*, the Easter egg being the cardboard sort that has presents inside.

Half the class sits in a large, egg-shaped circle. The other half crouches inside the circle and 'comes alive' as different kinds of toys or 'movement surprises'. The circle could be linked with a ribbon which the children hold and move gently up and down before the presents wake up. (*See 75.*)

Older children enjoy the idea of spring as 'awakening' or 'new beginnings'. Many folk dances from different countries evoke growth and fertility through their step patterns and forms and might well provide ideas and rhythmic frameworks for the classes.

Shapes and Sculpture

112 Natural Shapes

Visits to exhibitions of sculpture may spark off movement ideas. Ideas of, for example, widening, curving, interlinking, angularity. In addition, the natural shapes in the environment give ideas for body shapes, actions and relationships between people. As a movement framework, suggest the children move from one shape to another.

Shapes in nature often 'look like' something and children are quick to point this out. So ideas that emerge from looking at shapes may result in fantasy situations; for example, where the shapes 'become' types of creatures. (*See 97.*) Alternatively, the shapes may relate to mood or may stimulate abstract dance where there is no meaning besides that of patterns and rhythms. In any ideas using shapes it is important to stress movement continuity, shapes evolving out of moving rather than a meaningless series of poses.

113 A List of Ideas

Ideas which have started exploratory work on moving shapes include a mobile, a clay model, pebbles, sea shells, sculpture, parts of an engine, looking at buildings, flower designs. The dance work can be linked to making sculptures in clay, wood and wire.

Make yourself into a body sculpture. Move slowly and change what you look like. Work with a partner to produce a human sculpture. Use:

touching or supporting each other
leading each other
one still, the other moving around the 'sculpture'.

114 A Room-sized Sculpture

The idea here is a huge sculpture for moving within, around, over, etc., and it could be an impromptu disposable one. Nowadays many artists are exploring this idea.

Children can make a structure using chairs, cardboard boxes, tables, motor tyres and create an *instant sculpture* through interlinking these objects as well as constructing more permanent 'stuck together' ones.

Encourage them to look at the sculptural properties of everyday objects and to adapt their body shapes and movement to them.

Sound

Listen to the sounds around you. Use the surroundings as a source of sound.

115 Percussion Instruments

As well as accompanying movement (**9**), percussion instruments can be used as a stimulus for movement. The different sounds can imitate different ways of moving, using different body parts and speeds.

A cymbal suggests smooth turns, smooth travelling and arm movements, sudden leaps, sudden falls, vibrating, and collapsing. The shape of the cymbal could also be used to suggest group shapes or floor patterns.

Clappers suggest fast dodging from side to side, sudden movements of different parts of the body.

Suggestions for ways of moving can come from the teacher and the children. A lesson might be based on two contrasting movements. (*See* **220**.)

Experiment with playing instruments in different ways. Encourage interest in listening to and making sounds. Link with music lessons. Make group percussion pieces by combining and repeating sounds. Remember that percussion can stimulate action, accompany the action and be danced with. (*See* **214**.)

116 Homemade Instruments and Sound Effects

Interesting sounds can be produced by beating, shaking or tapping anything that might produce a sound. Use the environment as well as objects. For example, knocking pebbles together — pebble rhythms, tapping a stick on the floor or along a radiator, beating a saucepan, screwing up newspaper, shaking a homemade shaker, hitting wooden spoons together, stamping out rhythms on the floor. Dance and make sound simultaneously. Make a movement BAND to the radiator rhythm or the floor beat!

117 Pebble Sounds

For example:
Tap them high, low and all around the body. Make up-and-down and side-to-side rhythms. Tap them quickly while *running and turning*. Tap them high in the air while leaping. Or use them very *slowly*! For example, roll them very slowly with gentle hands, feel them softly with your feet as you turn them. Make a partner dance. One child dances with the pebbles near the other child who is kneeling. Change over with a slow, slow movement.

118 Newspaper Sounds

Screw the newspaper up with big, twisting movements. Make the crackling sound start and stop. Shake a sheet of newspaper. Make *whipping* sounds and movement with a strip of newspaper. Using big movements, slowly fold up a sheet of newspaper. Try not to make a sound. (*See also* **187**.)

Make an individual dance. Begin it by sitting quite still on a piece of newspaper. Tape record 'newspaper sounds' as a background accompaniment.

Remember to explore the movement in disciplined phrases of action. Each idea must be repeated many times. Sometimes the movement may remind the children of a particular mood or experience and this may be incorporated in the dance.

119 Body Contact Sounds

These include clicking fingers, clapping hands, slapping the body, stamping the floor ('play a rhythm on the floor with your feet'), tapping on the floor, smoothing the floor, rubbing the hands together.

Use one activity at a time to begin with — perhaps slapping or tapping rhythms. Stress silence and stillness at the beginning and end of each sound. Then encourage the children to *move* with the sound. Interesting sequences will arise if they then work on linking sounds and movements, such as a stamping, clapping dance or a slapping, leaping dance.

Mix up slow sounds with quick sounds. Contrast high and low movements. Make up partner dances which are 'conversations' in movement and sound. For example, 'I clap high and low. You jump and stamp your feet and turn with clicking fingers'. (*See* **212**.)

Sssnnnwhuffffll?

Hnwhuffl hhnnwfl hnfl hfl?

Gdroblbobhlhobngbl gbl gl g g g g glbgl.

Drublhaflablhaflubhafgabhaflhafl fl fl—

gm grawwwww grf grawf awfgm graw gm.

Hovoplodok—doplodovok—plovodokot—doplodokosh?

Splgraw fok fok splgrafhatchgabrlgabrl fok splfok!

Zgra kra gka fok!

Grof grawff gahf?

Gombl mbl bl—

blm plm,

blm plm,

blm plm,

blp.

The Loch Ness Monster's Song by Edwin Morgan from *Poems
of Thirty Years* (Carcanet Press).

120 Chants

Many of the lessons use chants as accompaniment. A chant is made by repeating and rhythmizing a word or phrase. Word rhythms can come from almost any source. A few of the possibilities include people's names, street names, railway stations, advertisements, vegetables or flowers, numbers, food, games, telephone numbers, graffiti, football teams.

Repeat the words or word over and over again until a pattern emerges with clear accents and pauses. This rhythm can then be related to any appropriate action. Rhythms with a strong underlying beat tend to be translated into feet or clapping movements. Non-metric rhythms (c a u l i f l o w e r) suggest body movements, such as opening and closing.

Also use *voice sounds*. Use singing and humming sounds with the lips and tongue to make your own music. Experiment with using words or parts of words. Listen to them as sound patterns as well as what they mean.

The following lessons use chants: Feet talk **208**; Stamping elephant; Humbug **215**; Rain dance **216**; Sausages and chips **213**; Names **211**.

121 Advertisements

Make a collection of advertisements from magazines or newspapers. The movement might be related to the meaning as well as the rhythm of the words. For example, *'Equal rights for wide feet!'* (a shoe advertisement) — make rhythms of small steps and large steps, feet in the air, feet on the ground or *'Let the train take the strain'* — a travelling step in a file, increasing the size and pace of the movement.

122 Songs

Many songs can be used for their mood or meaning. Folk songs contain a variety of rhythms and moods. The rhythm and phrasing of a song can be used as accompaniment for action. Sometimes the words and meanings can be used too.

Small movements of the shoulders, hands or feet can often be combined with classroom songs.

As with other stimulus the method is to select movement content ideas and develop these in rhythmic phrases, using the song as a framework. (*See also* **155** *and* **108**.)

123 'Oh I Do Like to be Beside the Seaside'

This song stimulated a seaside scene. The movement ideas were: clear *sequences* of travelling steps (galloping, hopping, skipping combinations) and *body shapes* connected to seaside actions. (*See also Ocean, pp. 137-143.*)

The children each worked with a partner to produce a unison travelling action. They then joined two other children and decided upon *seaside activities*, such as swimming movements, throwing and catching a ball, wave movements, shaking water off themselves, digging in the sand.

In groups of four the children made 'seaside pictures' by moving and stopping. The stopping was like a photograph of people digging or swimming.

124 Action Rhymes for Young Children

Chants may be developed in a dance or be used to encourage a particular movement experience in the starting activities. Chants can be used as a basis for directed or creative activities. For example,

> Jump-jump! Kangaroo Brown,
> Jump-jump! Off to town,
> Jump-jump! Up hill and down,
> Jump-jump! Kangaroo Brown.

Use this for jumping practice.

Jump all the way through the verse rather than following the words. Try jumps with the feet together or apart and together. Or jumps that can take you forward, jumps that turn you round.

The wheels on the bus go round and round, etc.

Other ways of going 'round and round' might be explored.

Nursery rhymes can be used in a similar fashion. Sometimes use the rhythm alone, sometimes the rhythm and meaning. Brian Wildsmith's *Mother Goose* offers a good collection of rhymes and illustrations.

Poetry

125 Poems and Dance

Words are used throughout this book, both to stimulate and categorize movement. Poems are one of the best sources for vivid word ideas. Many of the other ideas could be linked to a poem. Poetry and dance are very akin to each other. Encourage children to collect poems that they enjoy and to use poems that they themselves have written. The teacher might use the poem as a source of movement ideas for herself or read the poem to the children as a stimulus for their creative movement. Nowadays poems can be found in all sorts of places; for example, on the London Underground. They are read aloud in public places. You could write a poem on the wall and dance in front of it.

126 Introducing the Poem

It is important to decide how the poem is to be introduced. Some poems are too long or complex to be introduced in the dance lesson and should be read and discussed beforehand. Other poems are best used immediately and spontaneously during the lesson. Sometimes basic movement work related to the poem is best worked on before the poem is introduced.

Assess the most suitable method. Aim for a clear dance response with every part of the body fully extended and participating. Evaluate what aspect of the poem will stimulate this response. The dance will usually reflect the mood of the poem, although not slavishly interpreting it.

127 Poem and Accompaniment

Words or phrases from the poem can be used as a rhythmic or qualitative accompaniment. The mood or images may suggest a particular type of voice sound or percussion accompaniment — smooth and quiet or loud and vigorous.

It is also possible to divide up a longer poem in the following way: a part of it is spoken; a part is selected for development into dance; and a part initiates a short percussion or sound piece. These are a few of the many possibilities of linking words, sounds and movement in very simple ways. Mix up movement, words and sounds.

Give one of the poems on page 69 to each group.
Move to the rhythm.
Move from the image.
Keep it very simple and fun!

The two knock knock examples from,
Knock Knocks by William Cole (Grafton Books, a division of Wm. Collins Sons and Co. Ltd.)

Ode to a Goldfish

O
Wet
Pet

Gyles Brandreth

The Tickle Rhyme

'Who's that tickling my back?'
said the wall
'Me,' said a small caterpillar
'I'm learning to crawl.'
Ian Serraillier

Peter Piper picked
a peck of pickled pepper.
A peck of pickled pepper
Peter Piper picked.
(FAST OR SLOW)

Knock knock.
Who's there?
Moppet
Moppet who?
Moppet, up
before it
gets sticky!

Fuzzy Wuzzy was a bear
Fuzzy Wuzzy had no hair
Fuzzy Wuzzy wasn't fuzzy
was he?

Knock knock
Who's there?
Justin.
Justin who?
Just in time for dinner!

128 Selecting Movement Content

Select a few ideas and a limited movement framework for those ideas. Do not try to perform an enactment of a whole poem, but select words or phrases as starting points to action.

Some words will stimulate actual actions (jump, twist). Some will suggest *how* to move (slowly, suddenly). Others will suggest a mood or atmosphere.

Others can be used as a rhythm. Play the rhythm on a percussion instrument without the words. Never use a poem for movement until the children are warmed up mentally and physically, responsive to listening and moving. Avoid lengthy discussions. Listen, select, move.

See also the poems used in Part 3, and the **Ocean** section (p. *137-143*) for poems written by children.

129 'On the Ning Nang Nong'

> On the Ning Nang Nong
> Where the Cows go Bong!
> And the Monkeys all say Boo!
> There's a Nong Nang Ning
> Where the trees go Ping!
> And the tea-pots Jibbet Jabbet Joo.
> On the Nong Ning Nang
> All the mice go Clang!
> And you just can't catch 'em when they do!
> So it's Ning Nang Nong
> Cows go Bong!
> Nong Nang Ning!
> Trees go Ping!
> Nong Ning Nang!
> The mice go Clang!
> What a noisy place to belong,
> Is the Ning Nang Ning Nang Nong.

by Spike Milligan in *Rhyme and Rhythm — Blue Book* (Gibson and Wilson)

This is another poem where the words can be used as accompaniment. 'Ning Nang Nong' is obviously a mad place. Use the words 'clang', 'bong' and 'ping'. Relate the words to action.

The children could say and move the words in a number or strange ways. Perhaps 'Ning Nang Nong', strange walks, strange jumps, or strange arm gestures. Again one line might be chosen for a unison class action.

Stories

130 Story to Movement

Existing stories can be good sources of movement ideas if it is remembered that rhythm and action movement quality and relationships, rather than mime, are the basic materials of dance. Many of the ideas in this book could be related to a specific story or situation if the teacher so wished. For example, the Tunnel lesson might be used with the Greek myth, 'The Minotaur in the Labyrinth', or red crêpe-paper streamers used to symbolize fire in a 'Fire of London' dance. The exploration in dance terms would remain the same.

Look around the classroom and choose stories suitable for dance. Remember to sectionize; pick out or provide action words; provide rhythmic accompaniment; consider the dance form. (*See also page 62.*)

The following story illustrates the selecting of movement ideas from a mass of detail.

131 The Pied Piper Story

This story can be used to show the movement of the people and the movement of the rats. One group of children did not attempt to dance the whole story. They danced selected ideas and the rest was shown by a series of paintings. The following sequences were worked on in rhythmic phrases, interspersed with showing paintings.

The rats — hide, peep out, zig-zag.
The people — dodge, jump up in the air as they chased or avoided rats.
The rats — follow my leader skipping, tumble down and drown.
The people — clapping, skipping, meeting and parting, then sinking slowly and sadly down.

132 An Enormous Dragon

He lives alone in the forest. He is dark green in colour and eats berries and leaves. Sometimes he travels down to the nearby village. All the people are very frightened and run away and hide until he leaves. Really, he is a very friendly dragon and only wants some company. He sits down in the square and cries. The people approach him carefully and gradually realize that he will not harm them. They also discover that he is a very warm creature who is nice to snuggle up to, and will always blow some warmth into their houses. Soon he is living happily in the village with all the people.

This is a shortened version of a story made up by a group of children. The story could be acted out as a mime. To bring about a dance experience, certain action words must be selected as a basis for movement invention:

The dragon — slithers, leaps, lashes.
The people — listen, run, hide.

Each of these actions must be phrased and made dance-like, using perhaps level direction and body shape in the development.

Half the class might perform dragon-type movements, while the other half performs as the people.

Accompaniment One class used the word 'enormous' as accompaniment for their large movements. Use a cymbal for the dragon and tambour beats for the people.

133 Making Up a Story from Movement Words

Here, the method is to select and develop suitable contrasting movements and then add imagery to the movement. The imagery should make the movement more vivid, not detract from it.

For example, first explore the movements: rush, struggle, crawl, balance. Then ask, 'Where might we be when we make these movements?' Imagery of forests, quicksands or ruined houses might arise. In using this approach for the first time, the teacher might have to provide the imagery, but children are usually quick to offer ideas which the movement has suggested to them.

This method sometimes gives more scope for creativity in imagery and movement than using an existing story, but either may provide a valid starting point.

Use newspapers, magazines and topical events as story sources. Select action words as a basis of the story sequence. Use repetitions as stories often do and change the stories too, to suit your own purposes. For example:

> In the News
> The Marathon
> Disaster
> A Day in the Life of . . .

134 A Dream — A Fantasy of Body Parts

This can evolve by experimenting with strange movement of different body parts. Quick or slow movements can be explored.

For example 'What happens to us in our dream?' In the dream our legs are very, very long. We stride with enormous steps. Our arms start twisting and turning like snakes, up and down. They get knotted together. We pull them apart. Our legs turn to rubber. We bounce about into strange shapes. Our heads begin to shake, then our whole body. We stop suddenly. Then we begin to grow bigger and bigger until we burst.

All the movement can, of course, be defined clearly in phrases. This story encourages awareness of body parts, and many other variations are possible. This example might be a culmination of the children's ideas or be used as an initial example to stimulate their creativity. (*See 16.*)

135 The Magic Carpet

Many stories for infants and juniors are about magical happenings. Again, select extracts from the story rather than trying to express the whole story in movement. For example, Mr Leakey is a magician who travels the world on a magic carpet and encounters strange situations and characters en route. (This story is *My Friend Mr Leakey* by J.B.S. Haldane.)

Use movement phrases arising from:

The magic carpet ride (in place) — rise and sink with gentle floating movements up and down. Balance on different body parts. Roll off as the carpet lands in, for example:

the *Land of Serpents* — use writhing and wriggling, rising and sinking, travelling along the ground fast on the stomach, back or side.

Ride off on the carpet again and land in the land of giants. Use huge, stamping strides, large, jumping turns, huge arm gestures.

Ride off on the carpet and land . . . etc.
Use any ideas which will give movement contrasts, such as volcano land, no gravity, whirlpool, a sad land.

Infant children could alternate between moving near and with the teacher for the magic carpet ride and moving on their own in their own space for the different lands. Juniors enjoy creating sequences in groups. Each group depicts a 'land'. All the groups join together in a unison sequence for the magic carpet ride.

136 Magic Words

When chanted and repeated as word rhythms, these are another movement source:

Salamandino!

> say it many times. Then move to:
> clap it
> stamp it
> jump it
> travel it.

Each group can work on different magic words, finding ways of moving together and varying the *quality* of both movement and sound.

The dance could end with the children deciding what *happens* to them as a result of the magic words. (*See 120.*)

For example, sit in a circle. Each child in turn says briefly what he would like the magic word to do for him. Ideas might be serious, playful, energetic, sad. A ritual feeling is added to this idea if a 'magic object' is passed around at the same time. When you receive it (for example, a percussion instrument, a pebble) it is your turn to speak.

137 The Four Gods (China)

This is a colourful story from the *Larousse Encyclopedia of Mythology*. Each year the numerous gods and goddesses assembled before the greatest of the gods, the August Personage of Jade. They would report on their activities and he would either praise or rebuke them.

Method
Four gods are selected. Each can be characterized by a particular way of moving.

The Moon Goddess begins in a curved body shape. She dances lightly, tracing curves in the air with her fingertips, on a curving floor pattern.

The Thunder God alternates strong, thrusting arm movements with stamping leaps and strongly held positions.

The Whirlwind God whirls in place and makes huge circles on the floor.

The Dragon God uses big whipping movements, sudden turns and sudden stops.

Group formation
Each type might be characterized by a group of children. The group formation could be a circle, a line, a loose group, etc.

For example, *Thunder God Group* — a circle. Alternate children leap into the centre and out again.

Suggested accompaniment — a different percussion sound for each group. Alternatively, Chinese music might be played quietly as a background for the movement.

138 Hand Shapes with Chinese Music

The music could also be used to stimulate another dance based on hand shapes and patterns which are formed very lightly and delicately (like Chinese paintings). Holding the hands well in front of the body, touch together different parts of the hands and see what shapes you make; little finger to thumb; back of the wrist to the front of the wrist; twist the wrists.

Make a dance based on a simple follow-my-leader travelling step to arrive in group shapes where the hands are important.

Masks and tunics
Masks and dragon-emblazoned tunics can be made. One class symbolized the August Personage by a huge picture of him, painted on cloth, and pinned on a wall as a focus for the whole idea.

139 Ravana the Demon King

In October/November the Hindu Divali Festival is celebrated in a variety of ways with story, music and the making of beautiful designs. Through dance we can focus on the story of King Rama and his wife Sita, who was stolen away by the demon Ravana.

In the forest — the pursuers — King Rama's group travelling carefully and quietly with movements of stepping over, pushing through, ducking under, waiting and watching positions, sudden leaps and stops, as they move through the forest searching for Sita and Ravana. This could be arranged in twos; one leads, the other follows.

Ravana and the demons — huge leaps accenting fierce fingers and legs, fierce arm gestures with the lower body held very firmly; short, menacing runs forward, finishing in a threatening position.

Make clear sequences of the above. Ravana could be in the centre of the group and Ravana and his demons could move alternately (question and answer format).

Half the room could represent the forest and the other half of the room the land of the demon king.

In this example only two main ideas are selected for movement. Beware of including so much story detail that the movement experience is lost.

Of course, a short slow-motion battle could finish the whole thing off and make a dream-like end with the rest of the story being read against the movement.

The pursuer and
the demons in
the forest.

140 Maui and the Sun (New Zealand)

'How Maui made the sun slow down' (from *Maori Myths and Tribal Legends*) relates how the sun was thought to rise each morning from a deep pit. The days were short because the sun crossed the sky too quickly and so Maui and his brothers decided upon a plan that would slow the sun down and make the days longer. They travelled cautiously by night until they came to the pit where the sun lay. As he rose up they captured him, tied him with ropes, and beat him. The sun struggled fiercely, but gradually became weaker, and to this day has moved slowly on his course across the sky.

The movement possibilities are many. In this instance we select only the idea of the sun. (*cf.* the story of **Ravana the Demon King, 139.**)

Begin with a mind picture. For example:

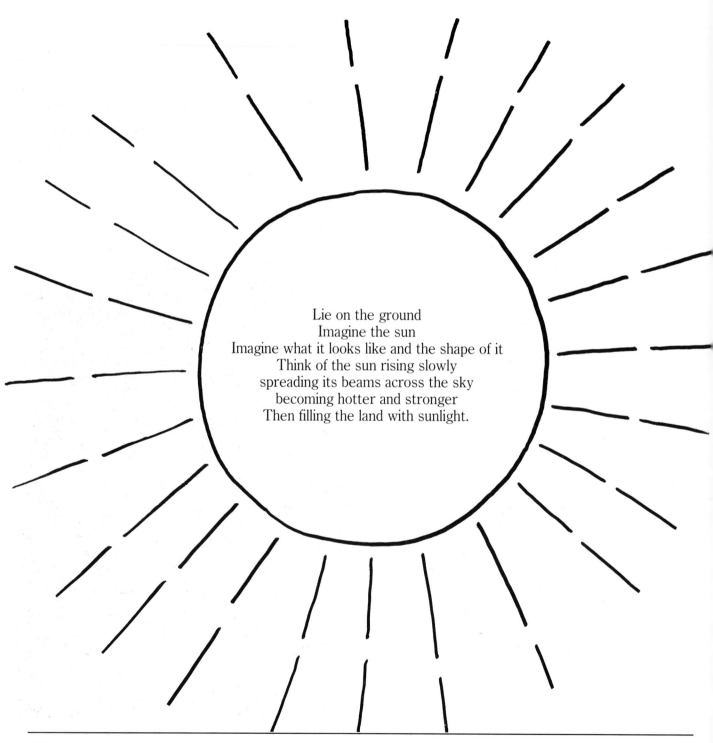

Lie on the ground
Imagine the sun
Imagine what it looks like and the shape of it
Think of the sun rising slowly
spreading its beams across the sky
becoming hotter and stronger
Then filling the land with sunlight.

For a short while observe the children's spontaneous movement from this image and develop the ideas emerging. For example:

> beginning in rounded soft positions, lying, kneeling or sitting
> stretching slowly out into the space, opening the whole body
> gradually, stretching and turning to stand
> leaping about the room with outstretched jumps and gestures.

Groups could 'grow and move' on this image, one by one.

Other elements in the story, the hunters and the whipping of the sun, might be *told* in story form or conveyed in a single phrase of unison movement.

141 Sun Follow-up Work

A large mural of the sun using and combining 'hot' colours in paint or coloured tissue-paper could be made.

The following poem, by a ten-year-old, resulted from discussion after the dance on feelings and thoughts about the sun.

The Sun

The sun came out
the moon went in
day and night goes by
the sun went in
the moon came out

The sun is hot
the moon is cold
hot cold sun moon
days go by
nights go by.

by Caroline Coles

Pictures

142 Illustrations

A good illustration can reinforce a movement idea or provide the initial idea. Look at the picture and relate it to movement. It may suggest the action of people or things, a particular quality of movement which can be developed. (*See also* **Movement Patterns, 67-71.**)

143 Sources

Sources of pictures are, of course, many and varied. For example, magazines, children's books, posters, murals, photographs. Take care to choose a picture which does have immediate movement associations. For example, a fairground photograph.

Encourage children to make collections of pictures or photographs which show different movements or qualities, to visit exhibitions and mural sites. Link *making* pictures with making movements. Arrange your own picture/dance exhibition.

144 Holiday Snaps

Bring these to school. Bring to life the actions, moods and situations that these snaps remind you of. For example, a lightning photograph which suggests fast, shooting movement of the arms, thrusting leaps, sinking down gently, stillness.

Suggest that the children move in sudden phrases of action, and then be quite still. For accompaniment, use a soft beating on a cymbal with occasional loud accents as a background to the children's movement rhythms.

145 A Collage 'Photograph' or Picture

Make your own collage both in movement and art work. This could be a group activity. Choose the subject matter and then each member of the group contributes both to the movement ideas and to the collage, so that the dance and the picture grow together. For example,

a football match with movements of jumping up and down, kicking, swerving, with an accompanying collage of cut-out figures, balls, team colours etc.

Suggest a dream design with movements of floating, spinning, slow motion falling, developed alongside a collage of dream objects and strange images. This idea could also be linked to the painting of a mural.

146 Television

Television offers an enormous range of visual stimuli. Current programmes may suggest ways of moving and can give a framework for improvisation. School broadcasts showing movement of nature or people might be recorded and later used as a movement stimulus.

An immediate way to begin would be to have everyone quietly focus, think to themselves about something they have seen on television. Then at a given signal they move and stop several times over, each using their own idea. Any number of movements may be observed. Help the children to clarify the *action* and *where* it goes in the space. Keep the phrases short. Everyone could copy one child's 'programme'.

Many other developments through *selection, copying* and *repeating* are possible.

Colourful Locations

147 Choosing a Scene

Choose a setting or scene as a starting point for ideas. The location could be 'in the news' at the moment. We can use real situations and events as starting points for movement *and* to explore issues. Avoid trying to depict all the actions within a large scene, but rather abstract some movement qualities or actions that will symbolize the scene. Remember, the narrower the selection, the greater the possibility of movement development. One advantage of using a place or colourful background is that other aspects of the child's work — creative writing, painting, etc. — can be linked to it. The scene might be shown through different media. Select simple actions, phrases and body shapes as starting points. For example, a ranch scene could be chosen where the cowboy whirls and throws a lasso and leaps and falls (from a bucking horse).

Suggestions for other scenes, inside and outside:

Jungle (*220*); Desert; Factory; Beach (see *123*); Oil rig; Mars (*224*); The city; Building site (*148*); Office life (*149*).

If possible, get out and about. Visit exhibitions, etc., which can 'transport' you in imagination to other scenes. Observe people working and playing in the real environment or move in an *imaginary* environment. For example,

> climbing over rocks
> rolling down a slope, etc.

'This looks very interesting. Try it in slow motion.'

148 Building site

Make a group unison movement from ideas of what builders do but enlarge the actions. Repeat in different directions. For example, lift and place, smooth, haul up.

Then everyone could practise an individual sequence of movements adding ideas to the above and perform them one after another in a line. Think of an ending.

149 Office Life

Visit an office. Observe the work movements but also the personal movements — hitching trousers, smoothing skirt, scratching head — office workers make. Or imagine an office scene.

Example 1: Typewriter rhythms

'Everyone tap out your own typewriter rhythm silently in the air in front of you. Make the movements very clear.' Keep this going for some time. Whichever group is pointed at, types. 'Now try tapping out the same rhythm with your feet. Work out some neat footwork.'

Partner work or one group moving after another could develop, together with sound patterns on instruments. Try to convey the 'business', the stopping and starting.

Example 2: Fast/slow motion sequence of everyday movements

> Sit, elbow on desk; scratch head
> Stand, walk, avoid, bend down to low shelf
> Stretch to high shelf, step backwards
> And turn.

Try the above very slowly, then very fast with large movements exaggerating the use of body parts and directions involved, adding more movements within the above framework.

What is it like to work in an office?
How does it make us move and *feel*?

Machines

150 Machine-like Movement

Machines can be a basis for ideas, but care must be taken to develop the movement.

The movement must involve and stretch the whole body. Begin with big movements. Stress the energy and power of machines. Small movements can grow later when the whole body involvement is present. Perhaps begin by making a machine-sound rhythm.

Visual stimuli are far more vivid then 'imagining' a machine. Look at machinery, such as a car engine, the inside of a watch, a home-made machine, a picture of a machine.

Ask what the parts of the machine *do*? Do they move up and down, round and round, vibrate? These can then be related to a movement rhythm and repetition. Ask what do they *look like*? Are they long, round, bent, twisted? These shapes can be related to starting body shapes of individuals or groups.

Try out lots of *different* parts of the machine in movement so that there is movement variety. Use different parts of the body.

151 An Orange-crushing Machine

The stimulus for this was a child's painting. The *actions* selected were bending, stretching with arm movements, leg movements, trunk and head movements — a whole machine body, circling, jerking.

The accompaniment was provided initially by clear word and tambour rhythms from the teacher; later, the children made voice sounds.

Each group evolved an ending by choosing to accelerate, slow down or get stuck.

The above example is rich in movement content. These ideas evolved with a group of ten-year-olds. Younger children might work on whole body movements to produce simple 'up-and-down' machines or 'round-and-round' machines.

152 Machines in Stories and Real Life

Children's stories very often contain exciting machine imagery. It is often enough to relate the lesson loosely to the story to spark off interest in the movement.

Contemporary life is full of machinery. How could we depict a computer?

153 A Class Machine

An exciting end to a lesson which explores different kinds of machine-like movements is to have the whole class become one enormous machine. What sort of a machine?

Method
The children sit around the edge of the room. One child begins in the centre of the room and establishes a clear phrase of machine-like movement. The next child comes beside him and 'fits in' with a similar or contrasting movement. Then the next child and the next child and so on until the whole class has joined the central group and made the machine.

Suggest the children all use a different body part and different directions. Perhaps add some voice sounds. (*See 51-53.*)

Work Dances

154 Occupational Actions

Traditional work dances are to be found throughout the world. Children can make their own work dances by observing the occupational actions that go on around them. For example, heaving, washing, cleaning, lifting, digging, chopping, pulling, typing. These can spring from locations such as a fishing boat, office, coal mine, factory, launderette, oil rig, house, building site. (*See also 147.*)

155 Work Songs

Many folk-song collections contain works songs. The rhythm of the music and the meaning of the words can be used for dance. It is important to repeat selected phrases of action rather than attempting to interpret literally all the actions in the song.

156 Sea Shanties

'What Shall We do with a Drunken Sailor?' and 'Pull Away, Me Boy' are both examples of 'hauling' shanties (hauling up the sails). A whole dance can be built on 'hauling' variations. Try humming the song. Without the words it is often easier to fit movements to the rhythm. Develop the quality of the movement and partner relationships. Haul together or one

after the other with changes of position. Half the class could tap out the rhythm and the other half could make some steps and jumps.

> Hill an gully rida,
> *Hill an gully.*
> Hill an gully rida,
> *Hill an gully.*
> An ah ben dung low dung,
> *Hill an gully.*
> An a low dung bessy dung,
> *Hill an gully.*
> Hill an gully rida,
> *Hill an gully.*
> Hill an gully rida,
> *Hill an gully.*
> An yu better mind yu tumble dung,
> *Hill an gully.*
> An yu tumble dung yu bruk yu neck,
> *Hill an gully.*

Hill an gully rida from *Mango Spice: 44 Caribbean Songs* (A & C Black) sung by roadbuilders with pickaxes.

> *Pull away, me boy, pull away, me boy.*
> *Pull away, me boy, pull away, me boy.*
>
> Jumbie tek all me money,
> *Pull away, me boy,*
> An he laugh after me,
> *Pull away, me boy,*
> *Pull away, me boy. . .*
>
> Jumbie tek all me food,
> *Pull away, me boy,*
> An he leave me to starve,
> *Pull away, me boy,*
> *Pull away, me boy. . .*
>
> Jumbie throw stone at me,
> *Pull away, me boy,*
> An he leave me in pain,
> *Pull away, me boy,*
> *Pull away, me boy. . .*

Pull away, Me Boy from *Buddy Lindo: Folk-songs of Trinidad and Tobago* (Oxford University Press) sung by fishermen about a wicked ghost.

Call and refrain
The songs above are examples of 'call and refrain' — an idea which can be used both in song and movement. It is much more effective to select one call and refrain. For example, 'Pull away, me boy . . .' and to repeat that many times over between small groups, varying the loudness of the words and adding ideas to the simple movement. For example, 'Pull away' one side, then the other or add stepping backward or turning *as* you pull.

The song or the rhythm of the song might form a quiet background for this movement and other similar phrases. Perhaps sometimes having an individual enact a particular line.

It is also possible to create your own 'call and refrain' work dance songs through choosing appropriate actions and rhythms and dividing the action between groups.

Games

157 Choosing Games

Find out what games the children play and assess whether they could be used as movement frameworks. Be aware of the symbolic nature of games as an outlet for moods and emotions. Games relate to playfulness but also to power, fear, the group, the outcast, etc., and these social implications can be used in the dance. Refer to *The Lore and Language of Schoolchildren* by Iona and Peter Opie (Oxford University Press). Choose games which give scope for variations. Many games involve complex patterns of skipping, jumping and hopping which can be linked to the dance work. Game ideas may grow into complete dances by developing variations, beginnings and endings.

158 'Feet Off Ground'

Run and stop when the drum stops beating, with feet off the ground. To vary, try lifting the feet and legs in different ways — feet high in a shoulder stand; balanced in a sitting position, arms and legs off the ground; lying on the stomach, 'flying' — lifting arms and legs.

The above game might be posed as a creative challenge or one or two examples taught and improved to strengthen the body and provide examples for future exploration. Alternatively, the children might choose what parts of their bodies are *on* the ground; for example, two feet and one hand on the ground, with the rest of the body stretching out. This idea is further exemplified in Musical Bumps.

What happens if you don't get your feet off the ground? In one group 'Red Poison' spread among them and they crumpled to the ground.

159 Musical Bumps

Children seem quite happy with game distortions. They serve to rouse the movement imagination. Six-year-olds enjoyed a 'sort of musical bumps', which involved bouncing down on to the floor on different body parts. Musical bumps that went wrong, perhaps?

160 'He' or 'Tag'

Organize the children into four groups. Two groups move at a time. Each group occupies half the hall space. Each group plays 'he'. When the tambour is playing they run and dodge. When it stops they freeze. Music can be used here.

Improving the movement
Encourage the children to make the movement very vigorous, to dodge, duck, retreat and stop. Praise skilful changes of direction. Each child must imagine that he is being chased even when he is not, so that the whole room is full of dodging, ducking, swerving children.

Practise standing in place and dodging parts of the body, dodging hands — up, down, behind, as if that part of the body is avoiding being touched. Do this with short, sharp rhythms.

Think of an ending. Imagine the 'game' suddenly becomes 'real'. What are you dodging from? What happens when you are 'touched'?

161 Imaginary Balls, Ropes, Hopscotch, etc.

Throw an imaginary ball from one to the other. This is a good exercise for developing response to others.

Practise 'Prepare, throw and hold the release position'. Vary the way of moving.

Make imaginary use of balls, skipping ropes, hoops hopscotch, swings, rocking horses.

Method
The teacher calls out the activity: bouncing a ball, bowling a hoop, skipping with a skipping rope. The children must respond quickly, with a change of activity and rhythm. Make sure that the movement is really well performed, extending the whole body. Work for co-ordination and flow.

Develop one of the activities by finding variations. (*See **172 and 188** for more ideas.*)

162 Hopscotch Dance

Jump your feet apart and together, apart and together. Turn on the fourth jump. Jump and balance on one leg with the other up behind you. Copy your partner's movement.

163 Grandmother's Footsteps

Practise different ways of approaching and different ways of freezing. It is a good exercise for quick thinking about ways to travel and ways to be still.

164 Box Game

This game involves the use of feet and legs, hands and arms, body, head.

Method
Paint a box. It becomes a movement dice. Print one of the body parts on each side of the box. With young children draw the body part. One child is in the *centre* of the room holding the box.

1 To a rhythm, everyone claps, walks, runs or skips (teacher stipulate) and STOPS.
2 The child throws up the box, calls out which side is uppermost as it lands and initiates a movement. Everyone copies this then — STOP. For example, the child calls out 'Feet!', begins to hop and jump then — STOPS.

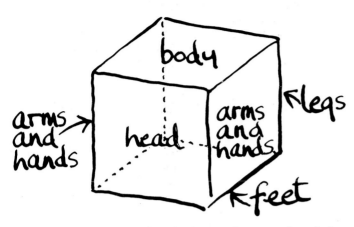

Change in the child with the box and repeat the whole idea many times.

The first time this game is tried, the teacher may need to throw up the box, then the children improvise. The teacher stimulates and improves the response. The aim is variety, invention. Adapt the game to suit the children.

This game has been used with great success by both younger and older children. The teacher may need to feed in the ideas initially. Each child has to be on his mettle.

165 Playground Chants

These can be used as accompaniment for movement by using the words and perhaps working out rhythm arrangements on percussion instruments. Any of the chants mentioned in *120* might be used. Some will be specifically from the playground.

> Mother in the kitchen
> Doing a bit of stitching
> In comes a burglar
> And out goes she.

Half the children clap or play. Half move. The children can work on skilful skipping steps which they relate to a partner, and then teach to another couple.

'Salt, mustard, vinegar, pepper' could be hopped, jumped, turned, etc., and sequences of foot actions evolved.

Playground chants often get louder or softer. The movements can be made bigger or sharper, can advance or retreat, so that relationships *between* groups can be worked out using the *mood* of the group chant, as well as the *actions* it has suggested. For example, a menacing group advancing on a quick light group.

Part 3

The Example Lessons

166 The Example Lessons (General)

The example lessons indicate:

(a) A selection of movement ideas related to children's experience
(b) the development of that material through examples, questions and tasks;
(c) the sort of dance that could develop

The *starting activities* which are an essential part of each lesson are listed under 24-33. Focus on breathing and/or relaxation *during* the movement and in stillness.

The example lessons are intended to demonstrate *growth* of ideas and are not meant to be absolutely definitive. Use your own colourful language and sense of timing to encourage the vital 'moving with awareness'. Used with sensitivity just *one* idea might constitute the lesson. For some teachers far too much detail is given. Always judge *how much* the children themselves can contribute. The ideas given here may help you to visualize a movement response or help you to observe what does actually arise in the lesson. (*See 22.*)

Keep the vitality and freshness of the movement, and avoid a stereotyped response. 'Asking in different ways' and 'Responding in different ways' are stressed. Some general suggestions are made for *accompaniment*.

The lessons give opportunity for *repetition* and growth of movement ideas in many contrasting contexts. Movement ability and awareness develop gradually over a period of time. The teacher must keep a balance between repetition and variety so that ideas are constantly reinforced and revitalized.

When working with young children the stress is on breadth of movement experience. Older children can remember movement in more detail. They can cope with more development *within* a phrase of movement, and enjoy creating and repeating impromptu dances.

Obviously there is much cross-sectioning possible between ideas. A few lessons are more suitable for older children, some for younger, but a large percentage of them can be used for any age group, by adapting the language and development ideas.

It is hoped that the teacher will *select* relevant dance ideas and tasks for her class, and also use the lessons as a guide towards planning her own dances with children. In each lesson:

> Remember to use
> **STARTING ACTIVITIES**
> **ACCOMPANIMENT**
> **REPETITION**

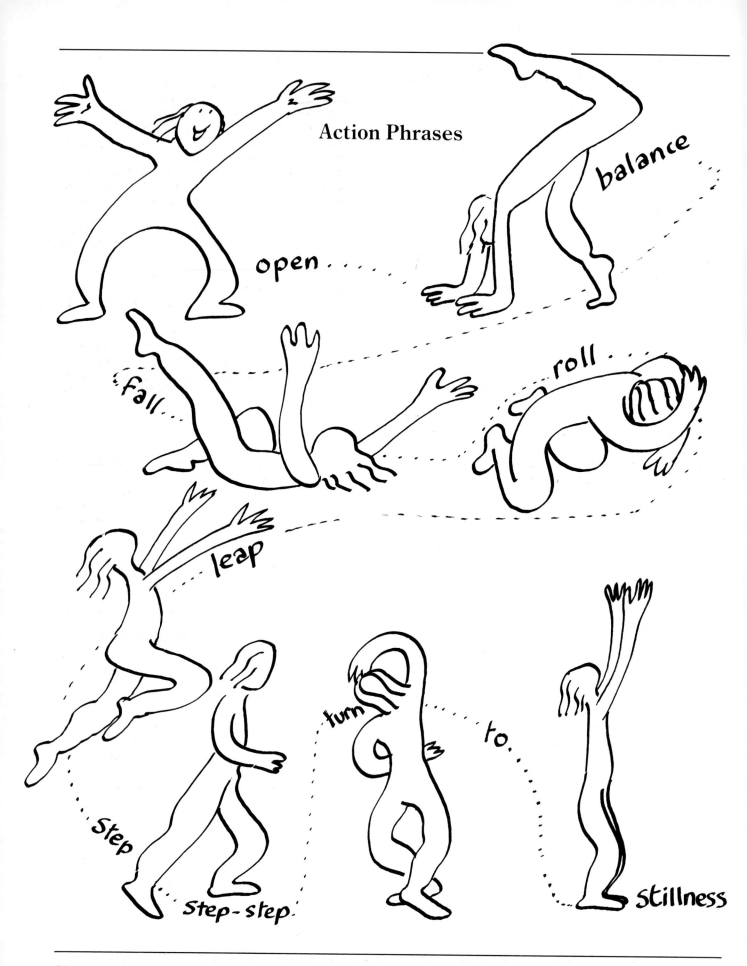

Action Phrases

balance

open

roll

Fall

leap

step

step-step

turn

to

stillness

Imagery and Action Words

167 Action Dance

Stretch
leap
roll, run
fall

These words contrast in place and travel. They stress whole body involvement. They can be practised individually or in sequences. The following experiences help build vocabulary and develop the joy of moving rhythmically. Task 8 'running' is particularly involving.

Follow up A group action painting from the ideas of running, falling, and rolling paint. Cover the paint with designs. Or make a movement poem.

Questions and tasks

1   Stretch one hand up, up to the ceiling, then sideways so your whole body stretches sideways, and then drops down to your feet. Bend your knees. And again repeat the stretch on the other side; stretch and stretch and down. Stretch and stretch and up, reaching for the ceiling.

2   Now stretching upwards quickly, shoot your fingers upwards . . . Extend the movement into jumping shooting upwards, really stretched, like trying to burst balloons above your head.

3   Now look around you for the spaces. Everyone leaping into a new space. Ready, really high stretching leaps: Leap, leap, leap, leap and balance.

4   Everyone copy that one. He's leaping from two feet back on to two, opening wide in the air (like a frog or Batman). All together: leap and leap and leap and hold the position.

5   Listen. I am going to play six beats on the Take all the six beats to lie down on your back. Think how you go down . . . Relax. Let everyth͟ͅ ͜o. Feel the floor underneath you. Lie quiet and still.

6   Curl up tight on your side. Now, roll and stop and roll back again. Once more. Ready . . .

7   Now roll and stretch up to standing. Who can do it smoothly and slowly? Good, I saw one of you stretch your legs, then your arms, then your whole self upwards.

8   Listen to the tambour. As I point to you, run quickly and lightly in and out among the other children and back to your place. Don't touch anyone. See how fast and lightly you can run. (Point to about six childen in quick succession, so six are running simultaneously.)

9   Now one person is going to run among you and past you. As he passes you, *fall* slowly to the ground and lie quite still. Ready . . . How are you falling?

10   All watch this one. Show them your gentle turning fall.

11   Lie down. Listen to the music. Think of the movements we have used. Use these, and any others that occur to you, with the music. Make your dance. Show me when it stops.

The dance
An individual dance
This may be very short, allowing a free choice of movement at the end of the lesson. This type of lesson gives scope for energetic, large movement, with very clear directives throughout. Older, inexperienced children find security in working in this way. Do not try to develop the 'dance' too much at this stage. Listen to the music more thoroughly in a following lesson.

Summary

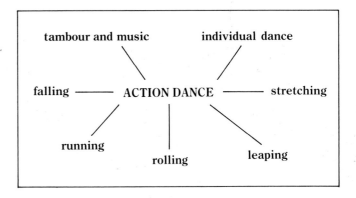

skipping turning dipping

The word 'flying' is used in an abstract sense to unify airborne movements. It could equally well be linked with ideas about birds. Note how definite sequences are given to develop the high, elevated quality. Once the children are absorbed *rhythmically*, variations will grow quite naturally.

Questions and tasks
1   Listen to the music. Move on the spot with large skipping steps. Step hop and step hop. Lift the legs; make the movement large, rhythmic.
2   Now move round the room. All go the same way this time to avoid bumping. Step hop and step hop and into the air and step hop. Feel yourself lifting up into the air. Push away from the floor with your feet.
3   Good. Now let's see a group at a time so that you have plenty of room. This time try and vary the movement a bit. Keep the *rhythm* going but perhaps *turn* it; or add arm movements or change direction.
    Good, there were some really clear shapes with the legs stretched to the side or behind.
4   How can we link these ideas to the idea of flying? Can you think of some more flying ideas? Turning with the arms dipping up and down? Using flying jumps in a group, interweaving or moving into the centre or out? Side-to-side rocking with wide arms?
5   Make groups of four people. Decide how you are going to begin, facing or back to back or . . .
6   Listen to the music. When it pauses, stop quite still. Notice where you are in relation to other people.

The dance
Small group dances
From a simple beginning many group variations will develop through: working in files or circles, intermingling, following or contrasting. Observe the response and help to clarify it.

Summary

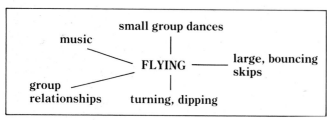

falling

Stress body shape and the *feel* of different parts of the body falling downwards. Use actions that *precede* and *follow* falling. Work with a partner. Use any imagery that arises, like 'falling through space'.

Questions and tasks
1   With the music try *collapsing* down very slowly. Start in a high, stretch position. Let the knees go, the elbows, the head, like melting.
2   Lie still for a moment. Feel really collapsed, heavy. Then *rise up slowly* into another stretch. *Balance* on any part of your body so that you are all in different shapes. And slowly collapse again.
3   Try now *spiralling* down. Open the arms so that you look wide. You could travel across the floor.
4   With a *partner* now. Spiralling down one after another.
5   What do you do when you are down to the ground? Roll and come up again? Leap up?
6   What do you do before the fall? Run and fall. Everyone try that many times, or leap and fall.
7   How could we make a dance called 'Free Fall'?

The dance
A partner dance
The children dance, sometimes at the same time, sometimes one after the other. They use the image of, for example, people or stars 'falling through space'. The dance might end with 'suspended' shapes or collapse (disintegration) of everyone.

Summary

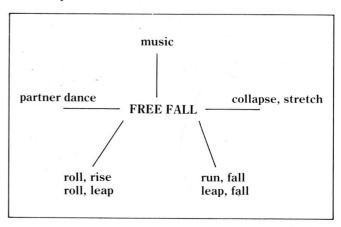

170 Nightmare

Talk about nightmares. How you feel in your dream? What *physical* memories do you have? These movements might be selected after an initial discussion about 'nightmares'. Use changes of *speed* and *sudden* stops. Stress *large* movements. Lie down or 'hang down' between each idea.
Follow up nightmare poems.

Questions and tasks

1 Begin by lying down. Listen to the music and *stand slowly* as if somebody is pulling you upwards. And stop. Hold your position.
2 Now begin whirling. You can't stop. You're caught up in the whirling. Dream and stop. Sink down slowly and rest.
3 The whirling goes on but *you* can't turn round all the time. Try arms whirling or head circling or running fast in a small circle, or a mixture of these.
4 Now begin to build whirling movements with your partner. Fit in, be higher or lower. Sometimes move *fast* sometimes *slow* down.
5 Yes, you could whirl each other. How does your whirl/dream end?
6 Now *float* gently up and down, to another space, like treading on feathers. And stop.
7 Follow your *partner, floating* to another space. Make the movements very big. Float the arm high, the knee high. How do you fit in with your partner?
8 Show me some nightmare *falls*. What would they be like?
9 Good.
   Jerking falls
   Spinning down fast into a heap
   Slowly crumpling, etc.
   Practise some of those with your partner.

The dance
A partner dance
This may contain contrasts of speed. Make the beginning and ending position clear. Make it clear whether the partner's movement is the same or contrasting. The teacher might help the children form a common plan, such as, whirling, slow-motion falling, disappearing, or the children could each decide on their own action order. They might choose *one* action only.

Summary

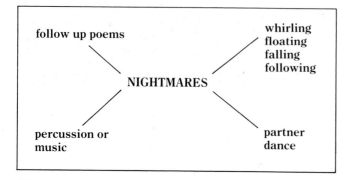

follow up poems

whirling
floating
falling
following

NIGHTMARES

percussion or music

partner dance

whirl

float   fall

171 A Procession

shaking clapping stepping

This lesson works first on *extending* and stretching the body. Then the movement is arranged in a circle and the contrast image of a gay procession is used as a culmination to the lesson. The idea could be developed further in subsequent lessons, perhaps 'stretching in the morning' and 'dancing in the night'.
Accompaniment steel-band music.

Questions and tasks

1 (Everyone kneeling.) Imagine you are like a piece of elastic and I am going to pull you out, stretch you into a shape. Ready? I pull your arms . . . then your toe *and* arm so that you have to balance, really stretch (etc.). Then change position with a roll.
2 Here's a phrase on the tambour . . . I want you to start kneeling, then roll and stretch out parts of you into the space into different shapes. Ready?

    roll and STRETCH
    roll and STRETCH

3 Good. Now remember one of those shapes and run and stop in the shape. Run and hold the shape . . .
4 Creep back to me . . .
5 Lift your arms loosely up and down and up and down and faster until you are shaking, shaking and stop. Try again. Begin with the arms, then let the body move, really *shaking* everything, up, down. Ready . . .
6 Sit near me and listen to the music. Yes, it goes with the shaking. And clapping? And skipping?
7 Half of you *kneel* in a space. The other half stand behind them. Those who are kneeling, clap your hands, and shake your shoulders and toss your head — really move the body. The others step and shake and clap, travelling among them. Make up a travelling step. When the music fades, stand behind someone again. (Then change places.)
8 Let's make a *procession*. Everyone sit or lounge on the floor. It's a hot day. There's going to be a carnival procession. I will choose one of you to head a file dance. As he passes you, you get up and join him, until everyone is dancing one behind the other. Ready — music — off you go!
9 Good, keep it going. Now see if you can stop, and *sit one by one* on the rhythm of the music. Sit and sit and sit and . . . (the music fades)

The dance
A file dance or dances
Use 8 and 9 many times over, encouraging development of a step pattern and shaking, shrugging shoulders and elbows.

Summary

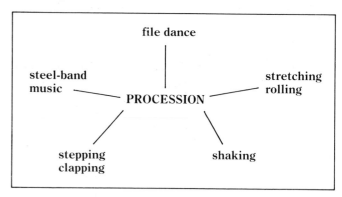

172 Skipping Dance

skipping

Develop and vary according to the age and ability of the children. Young children can only cope with 'forward', 'round and round' and 'to me'. Use cupboards, walls, other children as *focuses* for change of direction. Older children can cope with more variety of direction, more precise rhythms and more arm co-ordination.
Accompaniment folk songs, folk-dance music.

Questions and tasks

1 When I play the tambour, you skip; when I stop, you stop and listen. Ready, everyone skipping . . . really good skipping, stretch your back, lift your knees, use arms, etc.
2 Try skipping on the spot and stop. Now skipping and turning on the spot. Now skipping forwards eight skips. And then turning on the spot eight skips . . . Keep going forwards and then turning.
3 Here's a more difficult one. Eight skips forwards and eight skips *backwards*. Four skips on the spot and four skips turning. Use your arms. Find an arm pattern to go with your skips.
4 Supposing you make groups of four now. How are you going to dance together? Make up your own skipping dance. Ready . . .

5 Good. I saw this group of four moving two at a time skipping to the centre and passing back to back without bumping. Let's all try that . . .

6 These three skipped around in a circle with *one* child in the *middle*. Then they changed over without stopping the dance. Those four used *clapping* high as they met in the centre. Those four added a *jump* as they met.

The dance
A small group dance
This may evolve out of the lesson material. The movement was directed initially to improve the skipping and co-ordination, and provide directional examples. Then the children were free to discover their own dance forms, which in turn were noted and encouraged.

Summary

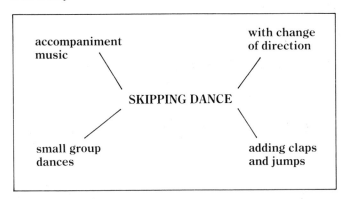

173 Swing, Leap, Fall Dance

swing
leap
fall

Accentuate the different qualities in these movements. Work for inner involvement, energy. Choose one image to draw one of the ideas together at the end. Work from movement to imagery. Use any images that occur. Each of the actions has been developed a little. Select from the ideas.

Questions and tasks
1 Face your partner, well away from him, and stretch your arms to the side. Now swing *down* and up to the other side. Swing and swing and swing and hold high. Make it flow. Let the swing take you as far as it can. Bend your knees. Don't be stiff. Let the *weight* of your body swing you.

2 Now swing your arms towards your partner and away. Move your whole body. Down and forward. Down and upward. Like a swingboat. Keep it going, higher. Swing yourself right off the ground.

3 Now make some swings with your partner. Hold hands, then let them go . . . swing with each other. Bring in jumps and turns.

4 Good, there are lots of different ways coming. Two there were swinging right over their heads; two there were swinging down on to the ground and turning.

5 Now follow your partner and do huge, war-dance *leaps* to another space and freeze. Ready, any large leaps . . .

6 Face your partner. Do a *turning leap* and hold. And turning leap and hold. Show me what sort of leap it is . . . Knees to the chest? A kick jump with the leg straight? You all look very fierce. Make a fierce leap dance opposite your partner . . .

7 Now, very gently, the first one *falls* to the ground, then the partner. I'll give you two sounds on the cymbal. And fall . . . And fall . . .

8 (Half the class watches. Half the class moves.) Once again, first one falls, then the partner. I want to see how many ways of falling slowly you can find.

9 Any ideas from falling? Leaves, aeroplanes, slow-motion diving, dying?

The dance
A pair dance
This could be based on any one action or a combination of actions. One class of ten-year-olds decided on a common image of leaves falling from trees in slow motion. They performed this very beautifully, spiralling down, curling down, stretching and falling from one leg. The falling was staggered — one pair moving, then the next.

Summary

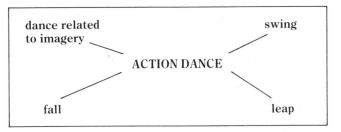

174 Tunnel

The children imagine themselves in a tunnel. In their imagination they vary the tunnel so that different ways of *crawling* are developed. They make a 'human tunnel' out of two files stretching towards each other making a long archway. Note how the other actions are only briefly enacted. Do not try to develop *every* aspect of the movement!

Questions and tasks

1 Imagine you are in a tunnel. There's no room to stand up. So crawl along on your stomach. All do the same movement to start with. Tuck one leg up beside you, the other stretched out straight behind you. Have one hand near your shoulder, one hand stretched out in front. Stretch . . . Now crawl. Bend and stretch the legs and arms. Really work the arms, the legs, the back.

crawl

slide

arch

4 Good. Let's pick out some of these. This one, on hands and feet. See how he brings his feet right up to his hands. Then pulling himself along, sliding on his tummy.

5 You're *out* of the tunnel! Move into the spaces. You can do all sorts of movement now when you're out of the tunnel. You can show me how you feel — choose your movement.

6 Everyone sit. How can we make a human tunnel? Suggestions?

7 The first two go and stand at the end of the room facing each other, well apart. Stretch your hands overhead to meet to make an arch. The next two go and make your arch in front of them. Good, your arch is kneeling, stretching sideways to meet. (And so on, until the whole clsss has made a tunnel which is two files with partners opposite one another and stretching towards each other in a variety of ways.)

The dance

A follow-my-leader dance based on 1-5; or half the class makes tunnels, the other half travels through them. Change over. Unison 'happy movement' to end.

Alternatively, each group makes a tunnel. The first two children travel through the tunnel and then join on the end of it. The next two travel through, and so on, until all the children in the group have travelled through. The tunnel collapses.

Summary

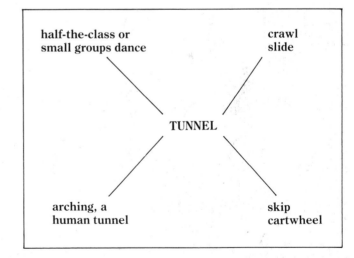

2 OK, you are out of the tunnel. Flop out on the ground for a moment. Imagine what *your* tunnel looks like — perhaps it is huge so you have to stretch and touch the walls, or gets larger then very small, or is slippery, or thick with mud, etc.

3 Now try going along the tunnel again. Try other ways of getting along this tunnel. Ready and . . .

Movement Patterns

175 Circles

circling
running

Circles can suggest circling *body parts*, a circle *floor pattern* or a circle formation. Use a brightly coloured circle pattern or design as a stimulus. 'What kind of circles can we make?', 'What do circles make us think of?'
Accompaniment pre-recorded 'humming' at different pitches and phrase lengths. (*See* **52**.)

Questions and tasks

Formation
1 In groups of four, hold hands very lightly, elbows a little bent. Rise up on your toes and let's see which group can *run* in a very *smooth* circle. Do it to the sounds we recorded. As the sound fades, slow down and stop.
2 Try the other way, holding very lightly, hardly touching. Ready, running lightly . . . and stop.

Floor pattern
3 Now each one of you run a circle *on the floor* and back to your own space as if you are making a circle of footprints.

Body parts
4 Each one of you hold out your *arm*, stretch it far from your body. Trace huge *circles in the air* around the body, like making circles of fire. Try the other arm.
5 Keep making circles with one arm, then the other, behind you, above you, etc. Make your circles *fit in* with the other three children's.
6 Make a circling idea together. You could use your leg or your head. That was a lovely idea. His head circled down to the ground as her arms circled *over* him.
7 How many ways can each group find of making a circle? Every time I *tap the drum* make a different circle formation. Good. I saw a back-to-back circle; a circle lying on the floor, feet in the centre; a circle falling with arms high (etc.).

The dance
In groups of four
Titles like magic circles, fire circles, flying saucers, hoops, might arise. Give a framework of beginning and ending in circle formation to a certain length of humming.

Younger children could work with the teacher in two groups — a circle formation with a group inside it. Alternate travelling *around* the circle with circling body parts inside it.

Summary

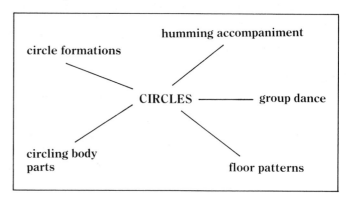

176 Kaleidoscope

moving
stopping

Look down a kaleidoscope. See how the particles move and stop in different shapes and patterns. Use the idea of moving in different ways, stopping in different ways.
Accompaniment a tambourine to stimulate the shaking of the kaleidoscope.

Questions and tasks
1 Stand by yourself in a space. Listen to the tambourine. Roll and balance high in any *shape* you like. And again.
2 *Skipping* and turning among each other. Use lots of changes of direction — in and out, up and down. And *still*. Try that many times. Every time you stop, you form a *pattern* with someone near you.
3 Practise sharp jumps with the fingers shooting high. Practise that sharp, knee-in-the-air, turn.
4 Take a *partner's* hand. Move with your partner on the spot. Move up and down, under arms, round each other, get twisted up together. Make a pattern together. And stop and shake yourselves apart.

5 Are there any more ideas based on what you saw in the kaleidoscope? Try travelling slowly. Now travel along among each other with *sharp* movements as if your knees, elbows or feet were made of sharp glass. Move and stop near someone.

The dance
A dance for three
In groups, the children intermingle and freeze. Each child in turn acts as a leader for the sort of travelling the group does. What do we see in the human kaleidoscope?

The dance ends with the children finishing gently in a variety of body shapes.

In each part of the dance the children should have a clear relationship to each other.

Summary

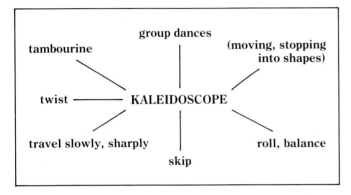

```
                   group dances
    tambourine              |         (moving, stopping
                            |              into shapes)

    twist ——————— KALEIDOSCOPE

    travel slowly, sharply     |         roll, balance
                            skip
```

177 A Pattern

curving twisting and giant steps

'It looks like a *rainbow*.' 'It looks like huge, different coloured snakes.' 'All different patterns together.' 'It's like giant footprints.'

Immediately after a dance lesson, a group of six-year-olds painted a large, brilliantly coloured 'moving painting', which was full of swirls, blobs and zig-zag patterns. Their remarks about it (above) were used as the stimulus for the next dance lesson. (*See Pictures, 142-146.*)

Questions and tasks
1 Who can make a rainbow shape of his body? A rainbow *curves*. All stand with your feet together and your arms stretched high overhead, and bend one way and the other way. And bend and bend and . . .

2 How else can we make a curve? Yes, from *kneeling*, curve backwards and then *curl* in forwards. Make a big rainbow backwards and curl forwards.

3 Hold your hand high. Now imagine you are painting those enormous coloured *snakes*. Paint them in the air all around the body. Ready . . . Up and down and to the side and behind you and to the floor . . . Big twisting movements. Keep painting the air full of snakes. And still.

4 Try once again. This time sometimes use *one hand*, sometimes the other. Try to go high and low.

5 Now half of you (i.e. half the class) stand still in your space. The other half are going to travel in among you twisting, turning, making snake patterns on the floor. Ready . . .

6 Now the other half. This time the ones who are on the spot move their *arms*, snake arms. The ones who are *moving* about use up and down as well as in and out — all moving and curving, snake arms, snake feet.

7 Lie in your space and stick a *giant* foot up in the air. Make it go as high as it can. And put it down. And the other giant foot. Good. Now sit up and make yourself as wide as you can, stretch your arms. Relax.

8 As I point to you, stand up and come to me with *giant steps*. Ready . . . And *walk, walk, walk* . . . And . . .

The dance
A short individual dance
Older children could make partner or small-group dances based on curving air and floor patterns, and words and phrases which are associated with them.

Many seasonal festivals involve pattern-making and this can be linked to movement.

Summary

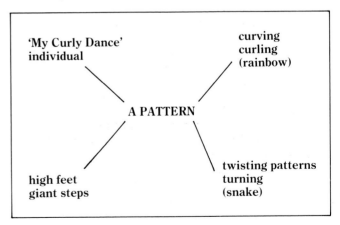

```
  'My Curly Dance'              curving
  individual                    curling
          \                     (rainbow)
           \                   /
            A PATTERN
           /                   \
          /                     \
  high feet               twisting patterns
  giant steps             turning
                          (snake)
```

Objects

178 The Ball

bounce
spin
roll

Summary

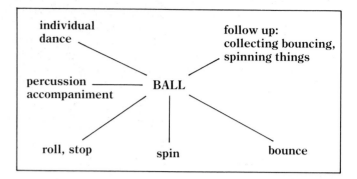

individual dance

percussion accompaniment — BALL

follow up: collecting bouncing, spinning things

roll, stop   spin   bounce

Note the development used in this lesson and compare it to 'Bounce and spin' (*208*) and 'Magic sound' (*211*) lessons where the same root actions are used with different development. This is the way movement progresses.

Remember here to use the *looking* at the ball as an initial stimulus. Do not dance to the ball's movement. This is too limiting. Make it clear to the children when they are to come to you and when to stay in place.

Follow up make a collection of things that bounce, spin or roll (e.g. marbles, sycamore seeds).

Questions and tasks

1 Watch the ball carefully. Whatever it does I want you to do. Don't *tell* me, *show* me with your body. (The teacher bounces the ball.) Spread out quickly . . . Ready and . . .
2 How many ideas did you have? I'll bounce the ball and then you begin . . .
3 Good, I saw high and low bounces and some people turning *and* bouncing. Try again. It might be a strange ball that goes tremendously high.
4 Sit on the floor. Now watch (spin it and *stop* it). Ready, off you go.
5 We had spinning on your *seat* but you could stretch your legs much more. And spinning on *one leg*. Can you lift and stretch the other one? Everyone practise that one. Spin on one leg (to the right) and spin on one leg (to the left).
6 And what else can the ball do? (Roll the ball.) Everyone begin to move a slow-motion *roll*. Really slow.
7 What can your *legs* do as you roll? This is a very good idea. All try . . . Start on your knees, roll on to your back. Stretch your legs in the air, curl up and roll on to your knees. Again . . . (i.e. clarify and develop the skill).

The dance

'Make your own "Ball dance". Use bouncing, spinning, rolling. Use other ideas you have thought of. What happens to you in the end?'

This idea arouses great enthusiasm. The older the child, the more the stress is laid on combining actions. An actual ball could be used in the dance. Fantasy could develop. The ball might have a magic power — everyone caught up in bionic bounces. Use the lesson's movement content as a guide.

179 Balloon

A variety of actions arise from *watching* a balloon. Watch the balloon and then make a rhythmic accompaniment with voice or percussion to practise phrases of action. The lesson demonstrates how the children's response is used in the development of the ideas.

Accompaniment tambourine and cymbal.

grow

bounce

burst

drift

settle

Questions and tasks

1 Listen to the sound. Start curled up and show me how you grow bigger and bigger and bigger and then smaller again. Lots of times.

2 Begin by balancing on any part of yourself. Can you grow much bigger this time? Perhaps your *leg* grows out a long way into the space behind you. Yes, all different-shaped ones.

3 Let's watch the balloon (inflated), and see how it goes along. Yes, it's *bouncing* very lightly. Half of you sit down in a space. The other half are going to bounce in the spaces among you very lightly, full of air. The sitting ones, bounce your *fingertips* on the floor. Ready . . . (then change over).

4 Could you all bounce in different shapes like different-shaped balloons?

5 Now everyone in a space, show me any balloon shape. Let the balloon sway a little, very gently. Now I'm going to BURST you!
Let's try that again. You burst very suddenly, and you land up still. Ready . . .

6 Good, some people are leaping, spinning or collapsing as they burst. Who is going to show us their bursting action?

7 Now start near me. You're my bunch of balloons — all different shapes. You're so light I am going to *blow you* away. As I blow you, *drift* into a space and settle there. (Blow a few at a time.) Practise drifting and floating.

8 Now slowly, slowly, I let your air out . . . down you go, gently to the ground.

The dance

The children can provide a simple story framework — perhaps the balloons are blown up lots of times before they stay up. They bounce gently around the room. They burst and all the pieces lie still.

Older children enjoy stretching into balloon shapes with a partner so that the movement is continuous, involving balancing, arching and rolling skills. One partner can inflate the other one!

The *sound* a balloon makes as it rapidly deflates, and the movement of travelling quickly (with rolling, tumbling or turning) to another spot, might also be used.

Remember to stress *quality* of movement. Take time to develop the response.

Summary

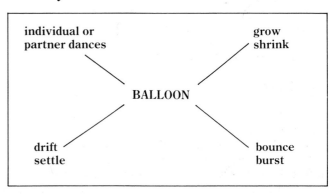

individual or partner dances

grow
shrink

BALLOON

drift
settle

bounce
burst

180 Dancing with a Balloon

toss
catch
run
leap

Summary

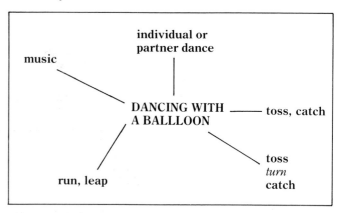

Dance *with* the balloon here. Demonstrate with one or two children how to hold the balloon firmly *far* from the body, so the body is stretched. Stress the use of the back. The balloon must be *followed* by the body stretching, bending and twisting. Stress the *quality* of the balloon through sensitivity to where it touches the body.

Have one group moving at a time.

Questions and tasks

1 Hold your balloon far from you to one side. Now *toss* it lightly upwards (keep hold of the string) and let it float down, then *toss* it again. Toss . . . and catch, and toss . . . and catch.

2 Make your whole body go upwards as you toss, and then sink down. Follow the movement of the balloon. Catch it gently on different parts of your body.

3 Good, I saw a knee and hand toss upwards too. Make the whole body join in. Try toss and touch now with the music. As the music fades, sink downwards and hold your balloon.

4 Space well out. Hold the balloon in your hands. Now throw it up gently and catch it gently. Sink downwards with the balloon. Feel how light it is. (Each group has a turn.)

5 Now throw it, turn under it and catch it. Throw . . . turn and catch, or turn, clap and catch. Try not to let the balloon touch the ground.

6 Good, I can see some lovely, smooth sequences of movement.

The dance

1 *An individual dance* to music. Show me how your dance begins. Show me where it goes in the space and how it ends.

2 *Partners* who must 'share' one balloon, one still and one moving, or one dancing with the balloon and one 'echoing' the movement. Another idea is to keep the balloon high by tapping it up gently with the hand, elbow, knee, head, etc.

181 Boxes

lift, skip
crouch, peep
jump
travel in

Use short, controlled phrases. Stress moving carefully. Half the class moves at a time. A story idea may develop. How can we use this box for movement? What ideas does it give us?

Accompaniment drumming, or quiet music, percussion.

Questions and tasks

1 *Lift* the box *high* above your head and *place it down* beside you, high above and place it down the other side. Treat it like something precious. Bend and stretch as you move it. How else can you lift it?

2 Light travelling now, between and around the boxes. Make sure you don't touch them.

3 And *crouch behind* a box. Hide behind as though it were sheltering you.

4 As I tap the woodblock, *peep* one bit of you out. It might be a *hand*, a *head*, a *foot* that comes out of hiding, and then goes back in again. Practise moving away from your box and then crouching again behind it. Make your movement clear.

5 And JUMP out from behind your box.

6 Other ideas might include jumping in and out of boxes, or moving *along* with or in the box.

Boxes

The dance

A half-the-class dance

The first half dances with the boxes. Each child makes his own dance with a clear beginning and ending. Then they change over. Make the dance short, to a definite length of music. A little story may result.

The idea of 'hiding' behind boxes was also used in a 'Pied Piper' idea. The rats hid and peeped out.

Summary

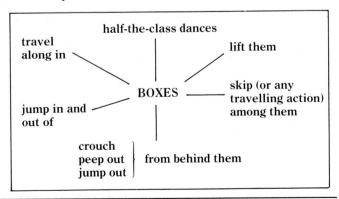

half-the-class dances

travel along in

lift them

BOXES

jump in and out of

skip (or any travelling action) among them

crouch
peep out
jump out

from behind them

Charlotte is a floppy rag doll and Jimmy is a simple, jointed marionette — pull the string and his legs fly up.

flop, stretch swing, tiptoe jump

The above are very useful stimuli for a wide age range. Obviously, the tone of this lesson is aimed at young children. Juniors have enjoyed finding all the strange movements and positions that Charlotte uses. In this lesson she is used for sitting with straight backs and for extending arms and legs, as well as being a creative stimulus for floppy movements.

Accompaniment young children — percussion; older children — music.

The dance
The individual dance
This evolved in 5-8. Older children would, of course, work on the dance longer and in more detail. Jimmy could be a starting point for *different* kinds of jumps (the ones Jimmy can't do as well as the ones he can!) in another lesson.

Questions and tasks
1 (Sit her up straight. Hold her head up.) Look at Charlotte. Look at her back (straight). Can you sit like that? And look at her legs (straight in front). You stretch your legs in front of you. Press your knees down. Press your toes down. Good, and now sit cross-legged.
2 Look at her *head*. It drops forwards, backwards, forwards and up . . .
3 Now I make her stand on tiptoe with her arms stretched wide. You do it with her. Really stretch.
4 And again and this time, tiptoe, tiptoe really stretched into your space . . . And sit on the floor.
5 Now Charlotte is going to dance for you. (Make the doll dance.) Yes, she's *swinging* her legs and *flopping* her head (etc.). See how she stops. Yes, she's got her leg over her ear.
6 Everyone show me a floppy starting position. Now listen to the tambourine play: floppety, shaky, shaky, flop sounds and you dance. Ready . . .
7 Those were lovely dances. I saw feet flopping up, and arms flopping round, Let's all practise floppy backs . . . and floppy hands . . . floppy legs.
8 Now half the class sit here by me and half the class find a starting position and show us your floppy dance. What funny position are you going to end in? (Change over.)
9 All sit near me. Look, here's Jimmy. What's he doing? Jumping his legs wide apart in the air. Everyone stand. Spread a little way away from me. Watch Jimmy and do four big *jumps* with him. Ready . . . and flop down to sitting. A floppy sit. And now a straight-backed sit.

Summary

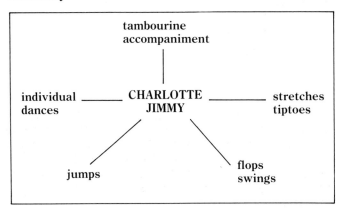

183 Crêpe Paper Shaker

shake
fly
swing
settle

Watch what it does. Move it for the children. Practise one idea at a time. Practise variations of each action. (The shaker could also be danced with. (*See* **78**.)
Accompaniment tambourine.

Questions and tasks
1 Watch it (shaking). You make a dance like that.
2 *Good. We had shaking* feet, hands etc. Everyone shake your hands high in the air and low near the ground.
3 Now watch it *fly* from one space . . . to another. Everyone stand, lift your heads up high, and FLY to another space, and FLY again and sink down to sitting.
4 Now watch it (swing). Show me your idea. Good. I can see someone there on his knees with a big side-to-side swing; someone swinging forwards and backwards. Let's practise some of those swinging movements.

The dance
Individual
You make your shaker dance now. Start lying down. Gradually come to life. Move, move and move and then sink down to the floor again.

Summary

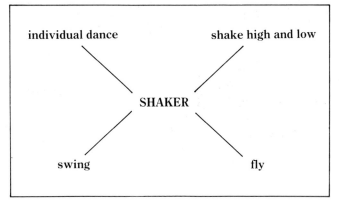

stretch, curl up vibrate, pull

Make the elastic move. Encourage the children to watch and copy the quality of the elastic. Later on, they could move with it, stretching and pulling, joined to a partner.

Questions and tasks

1 Watch how it stretches and stretches and curls up quickly.
2 Stretch the whole of yourself as far as you can and curl up quickly. Again . . . Try this from standing. Now from lying.
3 Watch how I stretch it up into the air.
4 Lie down. Whichever part of your body I call, you are going to stretch that elastic part up into the air . . . Your arm! Knee and hand! One foot! Two feet!
5 Now you choose which part. Ready . . .
6 Now stride with stretching steps. Move fast. Really stretch your legs to the rhythm.
7 Stay in your space. Stretch towards me. Can you balance on one foot? Stretch and let go.
8 Watch the elastic *vibrate*. I make it vibrate up and down.
9 Standing, make your hands vibrate, shiver, shake; your shoulders, your middles.
10 Half the class moves, vibrates, while the other half makes trembling voice sounds with me to accompany. Notice those who move every part of themselves.
11 Let's make a stretch line. Sit by me. As I beat the drum, run and stretch one by one, behind the other, make a long, stretchy line like a long piece of elastic.
12 Stretch it . . . And the elastic breaks!
13 Lie very still. Let all the energy go! As I touch you, stand slowly.

Summary

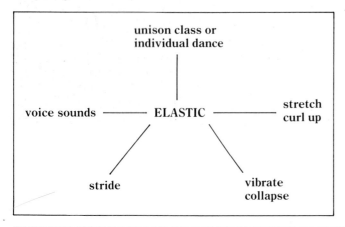

185 Floppy Frog

flop
stretch
jump

With the children gathered round watching, the teacher moves a bean-bag frog, using one movement idea at a time. The children space out and try the idea, then gather round and watch again. The frog is the starting point for invention and is not meant to be copied exactly. (*See also* **189**.)
Follow up talking and frog words. (*See* **Flash cards, 60-66**.)

Questions and tasks

1 Watch what he does. I pick him up and drop him down. Yes, he is *flopping* down. Can you do that? Find a space. *Stretch* up high and *flop* down. And again. Really *stretch* hard, really *flop*.
2 Come back to me. Watch what he *looks* like on the floor after I've dropped him. Yes, he is in a funny *shape* — his legs are over his head, one arm is spread out (etc.) . . . Show me your floppy shape on the floor. Now *stretch* up high and *flop* down and show me another floppy shape.
3 Come back to me. Watch how I lift him off the floor by his *toe* or his *head*, etc. I make his toe *stretch* in the air and *flop* down again. Make your floppy shape on the floor. Whichever *part* of you I call out, you *stretch* it up into the air and *flop* it down again.
4 Now he's tired of being on one spot. What is he doing? Yes, *jumping* from one space to another space all over the room. You do that, Ready . . . Let's practise some ways of jumping.

The dance
A little story
Frog is always trying to get off the ground and jump high, but he always flops back down again. (Or perhaps one day he succeeds and *jumps* away.)

Choose from some of the above ideas and accompany the action story with voice and percussion. Stress a clear beginning and ending.

Summary

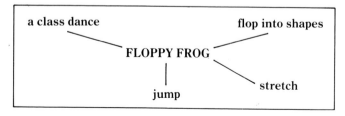

186 Leaf

floats
rolls
runs, tosses

Accompaniment tambourine or voice sound.

Questions and tasks

1 How can we use the leaf to give us ideas for moving? Sit near me. Watch the leaf as I let go of it. (Toss it in the air.) It floats or falls down. It goes this way and that way.
2 Kneeling, everyone stretch your fingers high and then *down* they come, this way, that way, this way, that way, touch the ground and stretch up again. Then do that standing. Toss yourself up and fall.
3 As I point to you, find a space and show me a big stretch up in the air as if you're hanging from a branch . . .
4 Now all together, listen to the cymbal (a quiet tap) and *float* down to the ground and up again. Roll right over and up again. Ready . . . And float, float down and *roll* and stretch up again and float . . . Feel like the leaf. Can you walk back to me on tiptoe and sit down very softly?
5 Watch the leaf. I'm going to be the wind and blow it *along the ground*. Watch what it does. Then half the class find a space; lie on your side, closed up tight. The rest of you sit by me.
6 As we blow, you are going to roll along the ground and stop. Ready with me . . . Blow w w w w, and still. Now we are going to blow you *back* to where you started from. Ready . . . (change groups and repeat).
7 I saw someone swaying as he stopped. Let's all try that.
8 Run in and out of spaces now as the wind *tosses* you into the air. Run and toss and run and toss. Can you get your fingers, your knees, high in the air?

102

The dance

Half the class sits in the centre of the room with the teacher. The rest spread round them. The group with the teacher 'blow', the other children dance. They float up and down on the spot, then run and toss to another space and settle on the ground.

Make a clear framework of sound for the above. (*See also 173.*)

Another idea would be to use real leaves. Go out of doors. Toss and follow them, roll and jump in them, or bring a few into the classroom.

Summary

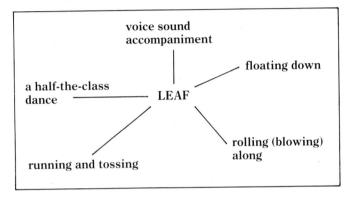

187 Newspaper

balance on jump over travel on

Try to encourage sensitivity to touching the newspaper with different body parts while balancing on the newspaper, and then a variety of ideas for ways of travelling on it. The *sound* the newspaper makes could be included in the idea. Stress choosing *one* main idea for the dance.
Accompaniment tambour, silence, newspaper sounds.

Questions and tasks

1 Sit very still on your piece of newspaper.
2 Move slowly and carefully (try not to crackle it) onto your knees, then to standing, then down to sitting again. (Listen to the slow beat on the tambour.)
3 Find out how many ways you can balance on your newspaper. Keep changing your position, moving slowly. (Yes, it is like being on a raft.)

4 Now stand beside your paper, and jump over it. Jump high over it; jump — turn over it. Try jumping very suddenly and stopping suddenly. Keep watching the newspaper.
5 Lie down on your newspaper. Think for a moment how you can get along on it: shuffling on your bottom; slithering on your tummy, dragging it slowly with one foot behind you. Keep the movement going. Stop when the tambour stops. Let's all practise some of the ways you have discovered.
6 For a moment, you decide on any other ways of using it. Start when I tap the tambour. Stop when I tap it again. Good. Floating it around you, jumping on to it, screwing it up so it makes loud sounds, wearing it on your head.
7 One by one, put your pieces of newspaper in a pile in the centre of the room.

The dance
Small group dances

For example, a dance could be built around three action words: balance on it; move over and around it; screw it up and leave it. Or the newspaper 'becomes' something — a raft, quicksands. This will be suggested by the nature of the movement, and the children's idea.

Summary

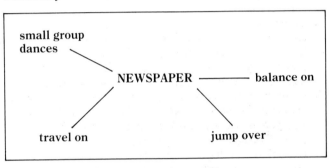

188 Skipping Rope

skip steps tossing twisting hopping

Summary

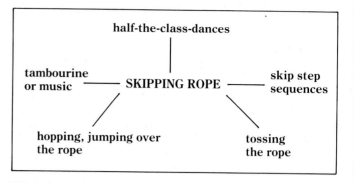

The rope is used in the hands, around the body and placed on the floor. Stress qualitative movement, the relationship *with* the rope.

Questions and tasks

1 Half the class sits by me. Half finds a space. *Skip on the spot* with your rope. Listen to the music. Use the rhythm. Try different skipping steps. (Change over.)
2 Now make *combinations* of steps as you skip. Use turning as well. (Change over.)
3 Good. There were lots of different *sequences* then.
4 Everyone *fold* your rope in half and hold it, so that the two ends are together.
5 Try *tossing and moving* the rope *around* the body, so you stretch and bend and turn. Keep it moving, up, down and behind you.
6 Try moving it with the other hand. Try from kneeling. See what different body *shapes* the rope makes you move into.
7 Put the rope down *on the* floor in a straight line. With your partner, *follow-my-leader* down the rope, jumping from one side to the other.
8 That was a very good step. All try that: step-hop, jump the feet apart, jump, land on one foot. All these ideas, and more, could be initiated by the children — 'brainstorming' with a rope.

The dance
A half-the-class dance
For example, put a pile of ropes in the middle of the room. One by one, the children take one and find a space. They begin to toss the rope in the space around the body, *twisting and turning*, rising and sinking. As the music comes up they begin to use the rope to *skip* with. The music fades. They slowly place the rope down on the floor. They then lightly bounce and *jump* over the rope back to the teacher. The second group goes one by one to a rope and repeats the idea. Alternatively, a partner dance might evolve.

189 Things

press turn

This works best with children who have some background in dance. One object is explored briefly as an example. Then each group is given an object (not the shell — see below) and asked to make a short dance. The teacher has to observe and develop the movement response. (*See 72, 73.*)

Questions and tasks

1 Come and look at these things I've brought along. Now start near me. As I tap the woodblock, I want you to run into a space and make yourself into the shape of one of the objects. See if I can guess which one you are doing.
2 Make the shapes really large so I can see where your legs are (where your head is) in the space. Ready, run and freeze. Good, masses of different ones there, some balanced on their feet, some on their shoulders.
3 Come and sit near me. Have a look at this *shell*. Yes, it's sharp with bits sticking out all over it. Could you grow slowly into that shape?
4 Curl up in a space and listen to the tambour. *Press* your arms, hands, feet, away from you into a balance. Press yourself into a *large, spiked* shape. And sink down again. And again . . . press, press . . .
5 How would you move along in that shape? As if the shell is being moved along by waves? That's a good idea. Turning from hand to knee, to seat, to hand, on the floor, stretching up the other parts of you as you roll and turn. (All try several ways.)
6 Each group now has an object. Put it in the middle of your group and spread out round it. Now all of you, show me a starting position that your object suggests to you. Good . . . and rest. And once again your starting position.

7 Now move in any way that your object suggests to you. What *actions* are you using? What *shapes* do you move into?

The dance
Give a specific time length (five minutes) for the dance to be worked on. Help each group to clarify and improve the actions and shapes that evolve. Stress flow, keeping the movement going.

One group used the 'frog'. They played with it and made it *move* — leaping, lying down, flinging the legs over the head, spinning on the stomach, etc. — and then evolved a flowing sequence of unison actions.

(Any one of these objects could, of course, be taken separately as a lesson idea.)

Group dances
These evolved from the actions, shapes and rhythms of the 'things'.

Summary

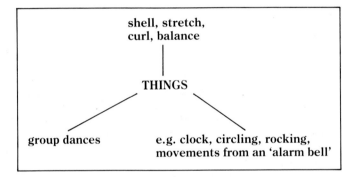

shell, stretch, curl, balance

THINGS

group dances

e.g. clock, circling, rocking, movements from an 'alarm bell'

Dressing up

190 Cloaks

open
whirl
close

The 'cloak' is a square of material held in the hands passing behind the back so that it is taut when the arms are stretched. The idea of handling and moving with a cloak can be introduced in the classroom. One or two children can try out the idea.

Divide the class into four equal groups. In this lesson the children move *without* the cloaks and then with them. This degree of control may not, of course, be necessary.

Questions and tasks
1 Everyone in a space. Stand with your arms as wide as you can, as if you are holding out an enormous cloak — very stretched, very proud and lifted.

2 Now imagine you are wrapping a cloak around you. Wrap your arms around you, close up. Bend your knees, tuck your head in and then *open* wide again. And *wide* and close *in*, and wide and close in . . . Use big movements.

3 Now step very deep, closing your cloak round you low near the ground, and then open out as you step *high*. Listen to the rhythm. Ready . . .

4 Who can bend right *back*? Curve back with your cloak wide and then *forward* to kneeling, closing the cloak round you.
Move with cloaks, one group at a time. One group sits about the room, well spaced out. The second group dances among them with the cloaks. The cloaks are then handed to the second group — handed very ceremoniously as part of the movement.

5 The children try the opening and closing movement with their cloaks. Make a dance with the cloak. Try opening, closing in, swirling round, using high and low.

6 Good. I saw some people really stretching, moving very smoothly using big movements. (Groups change over.)

7 The next group might try *whirling* the cloak around the body, or *running* with the cloak flying behind them.

The dance
A partner dance
One moving near, one still. Changing over the cloak. The stillness could be in a variety of positions. Perhaps the cloak 'brings you to life'. Many other partner ideas are possible. The relationship between the two can be evolved by the children or set as a limitation by the teacher.

In a circle, sitting
A quarter of the class is in the centre — statues ready to move, holding the cloaks. The children sitting clap softly and rhythmically. The children in the centre dance. The clapping fades. The children gently leave the cloaks on the ground and move quietly back into the circle. The teacher calls out the names of the next children to dance.

Summary

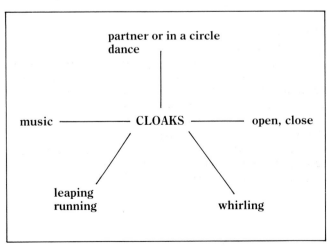

partner or in a circle dance

music ———— CLOAKS ———— open, close

leaping running

whirling

People

191 Clowns

walk
balance
run
fall

It is particularly important in this dance to stress rhythmic movement, and give both short phrases of action and short lengths of time for practising.

Quick line drawings of clowns balancing in different shapes on different parts of their bodies help to stimulate inventiveness. Funny shapes could also be used in jumping. The main emphasis here is on big exaggerated movements and slow then very fast movements, so that clown-like movement can be developed without recourse to mime, although the 'custard-pie' movement might well be a unison action which would draw the whole class together at the end.

Accompaniment percussion or a march, e.g. a march by Sousa.

Follow up make red noses out of cardboard egg-box sections and elastic, or make huge, newspaper-collage clowns, by tearing newspaper and making it into clown shapes in different positions.

Questions and tasks
1 Ready! Four huge walks on your heels. Four walks on your toes. What does your body look like? Can you do that lots of times? Listen to the rhythm.
2 Show me another funny walk.
3 Look at this picture of a clown. Yes, he's balancing on his bottom with his legs in the air. Show me!
4 Stand up. Every time I hit the cymbal you show me a clown balance. Ready . . .
5 There's a good one. Everyone try a balance on their front with their arms and legs lifted behind. Now roll over into another balance. Try a balance on one leg.
6 Mix up walks and balances.
7 Stand opposite your partner. Fall and balance. Take turns. See if you can make your balance different from your partner's. Jump up again after you have fallen.

8 All practise your clown movement — walking, balancing, falling and balancing. Begin when I tap the woodblock. Finish when I tap it again.
9 Everyone stay quite still in your balance. This boy is going to tiptoe among you. As he taps you, join on the end of his line.
10 Let's have a follow-my-leader clown file to end, walking with noses and knees high.

The dance
A simple class dance
A class dance might be developed from 8, 9, and 10 above, ending with a file of follow-my-leader clowns. Alternatively, the dance could involve partners rather than individuals. Older children enjoy moving in unison, building a short sequence.

Walking and falling
Use walking sounds and falling sounds as the framework of a dance. Half the class could play instruments and the other half moves, or one half could be walking clowns and one half falling clowns.

Summary

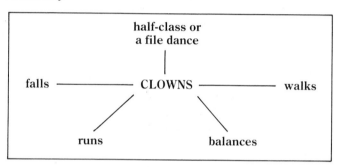

192 Fairytale Witches

twist
shoot

This dance is based on one main action — TWIST — which is explored through a variety of developments. Care must be taken to vary the speed and pace of the different movement experiences and compensatory movements of shooting or shaking provided to release any tension.

Accompaniment a witches' chant or music.
Follow up making costumes and masks.

Questions and tasks

1 Sit near me. Twist your hands into a twisted shape. Listen to the woodblock and change the shape. Shoot your fingers into the air.
2 Can you twist the wrists, the fingers, the whole arm, the body, so you are very twisted all over? (Use twisty words to accompany the childen's movement.)
3 Standing, try the same idea now, twisting quickly into different shapes. Use your hands, use your whole body. Ready and twist! Then shoot your arms upwards.
4 Find your own space and practise this idea. You change your shape now when *you* decide.
5 I saw some people twisting from high to low. Let's all try that. And from low to high. Try to finish with one hand low, one hand high.
6 All practise that twisting jump into the air.
7 Look for a space and travel into it along a twisting, turning pathway. Don't go straight there. Go this way, that way, this way.
8 Can you make your arms and legs twist and turn as you travel along?
9 Half the class stand in a twisted shape. Now the other half twist and travel among them . . . fast and stop.
10 Sit near me. Let's make up a spell, a very short one we can all say together. Move your hands as you say it.

The dance

A witches' circle
Use music for the dance. The children begin crouched in a circle. One by one they rise from the ground into twisted shapes. Then they intermingle, fitting in together, contrasting high and low movement. (Fade music.) They return to their places in the circle and begin a repetitive chant accompanied by a unison action (to symbolize pot-stirring, or making a spell). This grows to a climax and a suitable action ending is devised; for example, 'disappearing' with a leap and a fall.

Voice sounds
A witches' chant can accompany the movement. Initially practise the chant separately. Not all children are capable of moving and sounding simultaneously. They may lose all movement clarity. Younger and less experienced children would do better to use the chant only as an introduction or culmination of the main movement idea.

Summary

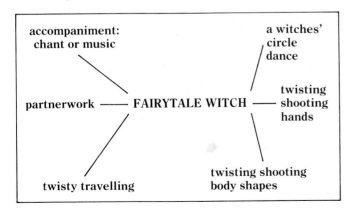

accompaniment: chant or music

a witches' circle dance

partnerwork —— FAIRYTALE WITCH —— twisting shooting hands

twisty travelling

twisting shooting body shapes

Moods and Emotions

193 Anger

stamp, leap, hit

Accompaniment cymbal and drum. Use crescendo and decrescendo.
Follow up masks can be useful additions to the dance.

Questions and tasks

1 Show me a really angry face. What do your eyes, jaw (etc.) look like? Change it and show me another angry face. Every time I tap the woodblock, change your face.
2 Stand slowly and make your whole body look angry. How does your body feel? Yes, very strong.
3 Change your position and with two big stamps show me strong legs, strong arms, strong head. Stamp, stamp hold, stamp, stamp hold. Make the strong shapes different.
4 Run and leap high with an angry face and body. Stop after your leap and hold your position. Run and *leap*.
5 Find a partner and leap one after the other. Show me some strong leap shapes. See if you can finish in a different position from your partner.
6 Spread out and hold your right arm very wide. Now make one big hitting movement. Now another. Now two together. Do the same with the left arm. Work on a sequence using hit, leap and stamp.
7 Stand in a strong position and then gradually relax until you are sitting gently.

The dance

An individual or partner dance
Try making an angry dance which begins slowly and gathers speed and strength to a climax, using the actions explored. The conclusion? A gentle sinking down, or a quiet return to the teacher with a simple unison action.

Discuss 'anger' with the children. What makes them angry? How do they feel afterwards? Show this clearly with movement and sounds.

Summary

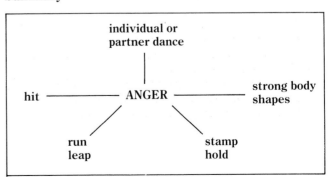

individual or partner dance

hit —— ANGER —— strong body shapes

run leap

stamp hold

Animals

194 Cat

stretch
leap
pounce
dash

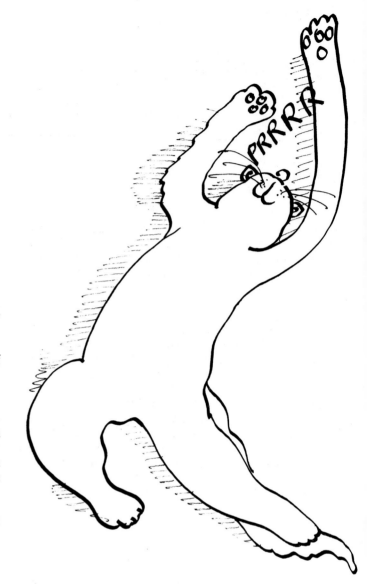

Remember to repeat each phrase many times, and accompany it with voice or percussion. Use cat sounds. Pssst, prrrr, yawns.

Accompaniment voice sounds and words, a tape recording of a cat purring.

Follow up cat poems.

Questions and tasks
1 What does a cat do? *How* does he move? (Select action words.)
2 Standing in your own space, stretch yourself into a curved shape like a big yawn. Arch backwards or curve over forwards.
3 Try kneeling. Stretch out into a curve. Try on all fours.
4 Now lie on the floor and curve yourself forwards and backwards quickly. Really move your back smoothly.
5 From your space, run and leap into the air. Stop suddenly. And again! As if suddenly startled.
6 What shape did you make yourself in the air? What did you look like when you stopped?
7 Everyone practise this child's curved shape in the air. See how his arms stretch up and back.
8 All practise leaping and stopping many times.
9 With a partner, practise a pouncing jump down on to the floor. Move one after the other. First ones — Ready . . . Second ones — Ready . . . Now all together . . . dash and hide yourselves!

The dance
A story framework

Cats stretch and stretch and jump up; leap high and pounce low upon their prey; run and hide themselves.

Each action is repeated rhythmically many times. The teacher's accompaniment helps make it dance-like. Then the children perform the dance in their own time (if they are ready for this) without the help of the teacher.

A poem and voice accompaniment

The children make up a short, vocal, action poem, making the words sound like the action, using lots of repetition. Half the class dances as the other half says the poem.

An individual dance

This could be based on the one word 'Pounce'. Make a pouncing dance to vigorous accompaniment.

Summary

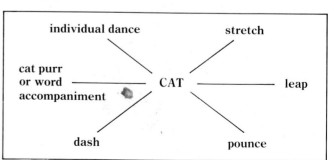

individual dance — stretch — cat purr or word accompaniment — CAT — leap — dash — pounce

195 Crocodile

wriggle
look
creep

This is a lesson for young children which might arise from poetry or story. Each movement is practised in short phrases, with clear going and stopping. The emphasis is on vivid movement sensation. Use the voice qualitatively.
Follow up a large, collage crocodile.

Questions and tasks

1 Show me how the crocodile moves along. He wriggles along: wriggle and wriggle and wriggle and *stop*.
2 Every time the crocodile stops he looks at me with his little red eye. And again: wriggle and wriggle and look (at me).
3 This is a happy crocodile. He wriggles on his stomach and on his back. Can *you* wriggle on your shoulders?
4 Creep back to me fast like a hunter in the jungle.
5 Now the *hunters creep* through the jungle. They creep near the ground and high over the tree-trunks. They stop and listen. You show me your careful creeping: Creep and creep and creep and creep and *freeze*.

6 Sit by me. This is the wriggling sound (a tambourine shaking gently). This is the creeping sound (tapping the woodblock). (Move with fingers only.) Then who can creep with the creeping sound? (Choose some children.) Who can wriggle with the wriggling sound? (Choose some.)
7 Only those children find a space. When I play for wriggling, let's see if the wrigglers can wriggle. The creeping ones keep *still*. When I play for creeping, the creeping ones creep and the wriggling ones keep still. (This may have to be broken down still more.)

The dance
The hunters and the crocodiles
Each group moves and stops accompanied by its own sound. At the end, perhaps the crocodiles go to sleep and the hunters creep back to the teacher.

Summary

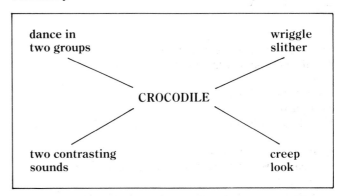

196 Monster

Enormous rising, sinking crawling slithering

Many different dances have evolved from these word actions. One class used the word 'Enormous' as self-accompaniment to the movement. (*See 120.*)
Follow-up work has included making a large monster out of boxes stuck together, and monster drawings which combine drawing and word patterns, i.e. making the name of the monster into a design.

Questions and tasks

1 Imagine a monster. What does it look like? Yes, a huge, great, long creature. It is very tall. Let's try making ourselves as tall and huge as possible.
2 Start near the ground. Now *rise up* very strongly and slowly. Show how enormous you are. Get as big as you can and *sink* down to the ground again as though you were appearing out of the mud. Again. Listen to the sound of the tambour getting louder and louder as you get higher.
3 Can you make your hands go high as you rise up?
4 What other part of you could lead you high? Good. I can see chests going high, elbows, head.
5 Rise up and sink down now, three times. Make the movements flow together. (Yes, it is like coming out to have a look.) Make a sequence.
6 Try rising and sinking with your *partner*. Begin together. Show me two huge creatures rising and sinking.
7 How do the monsters move along? Show me. Ready . . . One, two, three and four and *still*.
8 Make movements much bigger. Stretch out the arms and the legs.
9 Which direction can you go in? Show me.
10 Good. Everyone *sideways*. Now turning.
11 Look at the shape of this monster. Say he is covered in spikes.
12 Can you make a huge, spiked shape and change it quickly to another one? . . . And again. Practise this.
13 As I point to you, crawl to me and make a spiky shape.
14 Let's try again. Can we make a long, spiky shape out of the whole class — a class monster. Make the class monster by moving, one by one, to make a central group. Let's give the monster a name.

The dance
A class monster
The children rise and sink strongly in place. At a given signal, one by one they crawl to the centre of the room, joining on their shape to the one already there so that a large, long group shape is made. This can then travel and sink down to rest. This idea could also be enacted in small groups.
A partner dance
Make a very short dance about monsters. How do you begin? Do you move towards each other or around? How does it end? These questions help *stimulate* invention or *clarify* what the children have made. Set a time limit for the invention.

Summary

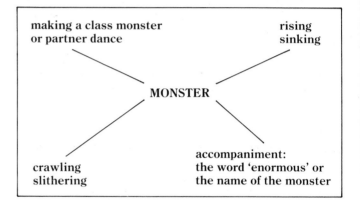

Nature

197 Birds

glide shake hop

Photographs of bird flight which show the different flying shapes help the idea, as does the observation of seagulls flying, converging, separating. Different types of birds — sparrows, eagles, penguins — can provide starting points for inventive and often amusing movement! (*See also 168.*)
Accompaniment use a cymbal for gliding and a woodblock for hopping. Bird sounds.

Questions and tasks

1 In place, stretch our arms wide. Listen to the cymbal. Turn and stretch . . . Again.
2 Dip down at your turn. Make one arm glide down, then the other. Bend and stretch as you glide up and down.
3 Now fly, glide stretched out wide to another space and glide up and down in that space.
4 Glide back to me and balance (hover).
5 Shake out your wings, really vigorously. And again!
6 Shake and jump up and down — like a bird in a bird-bath. Shake one side and then the other side.
7 How does a bird hop? He hops and stops. Try hop and stop three times and then listen. Turn your head sharply.
8 Where do you hop? That was a good idea — two hops forward and then some turning hops.
9 Find some arm movements to fit the hopping.
10 Half the class sits in the centre of the room. The other half glides and swoops around and comes to stillness and balance.
11 Half the class glides among the other half, who stand preparing to hop. Then the gliding group balance still while the hopping ones move. Have two sounds — cymbal and woodblock — to accompany.

The dance

A gliding and swooping dance
Half the class glides and swoops and the other half balances. Change over smoothly.
A sequence
Make a sequence of bird actions performed in groups or individually.

Summary

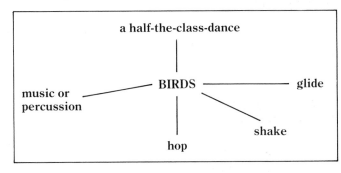

198 Rain

beat, clap run and rise

The excitement lies in the contrast between the strong, vigorous movement *in place*, and the light, *travelling* movement. The idea arose from watching rain beating against the window. Action words were selected from the children's suggestions. The rhythm of the *lesson* was fast. Movement *preparation* (e.g. rising before running) was stressed.
Follow up making 'Rain' poems.

Questions and tasks

1 Everyone in his own space. Rise up on your toes and . . . BEAT down on to the floor. And again . . .
2 Try beating with your feet (accompany with quick tapping on a tambourine). And beating your hands on the floor. Beat your feet on the floor and then your hands.
3 Can you beat your feet, then jump in the air? And beat your hands and jump in the air? (Otherwise the movement stays at a low level.)
4 Where else can we beat our hands? Yes, on our bodies and clapping high above our heads. Try that. Ready . . .
5 You make your beating, clapping rain dance in the air, on the floor, on your bodies. Lots of movement . . .
6 Everyone sit. Now half of you are going to run smoothly, arms wide, like the rain running smoothly in the gutter or down the window. The other half sit still. Ready. Run, run, run, run and rise, balance and . . . (change groups).

The dance

Two groups
This class might be divided into two groups, which move alternately. Each group has a leader. The teacher could lead one. All the children move on the rhythm. R-u-n and rise, *beat* on the floor, *beat* on the floor, stop. The second group begins as the first group stops. This idea is repeated many times so that one group is still while the other moves, but the rhythm is kept going. An exciting interplay develops.

Summary

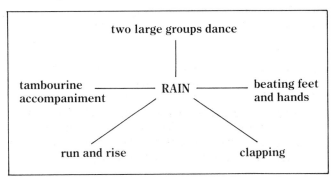

stretch curl shoot out

This dance contrasts sustained and sudden movement and group versus individual activity. (*See also 140.*)

Accompaniment percussion for the first part and quick, bright music for the second.

Follow up a tissue-paper collage using 'hot colours'. Build up layers of tissue paper and glue for a 'sunset' effect. (*See poem 'The Sun' included in 141.*)

Questions and tasks

1 Imagine, or look at the picture of the sun rising. What can you see? The light coming out — the rays of the sun appearing.
2 Sit near me. Clench your fists near your chest. Now slowly uncurl, stretch your fingers, your hands, your arms and slowly curl in again. And again.
3 Now I'll play the cymbal and you practise that. Imagine the sun as if it's inside you. Show me where your hands go in the space (some high, some sideways).
4 Stand, then curl near me. Slowly, starting with your fingers, uncurl and then stretch away from me. Stay there and slowly come back again. We are like the sun rising, getting bigger and bigger and sinking down again. Do that three times.
5 And hang down and breathe. Imagine the warm sun on your back.
6 In your new space let's think now how the sun shoots out its beams all over the sky. It's very bright now. Ready! Shoot your arms out and back again; shoot your leg out and back again; shoot one arm and one leg out and back again; shoot everything out and back again.
7 Listen to the sound. Show me how you shoot out into the space.
8 Stretch out wide like a huge sun and now slowly sink to the ground, down, down, like a sun setting. We could do that in one big group.
9 *Run* lightly, shooting your fingers and knees into the air as you go.

The dance

This can be enacted with the teacher, a partner or a small group.

Begin close to each other at a low level. Slowly stretch out so the group gets bigger and then shoot and dart into the space, leaving the group, sometimes travelling, sometimes on the spot. Return to the group and sink down slowly all together.

Summary

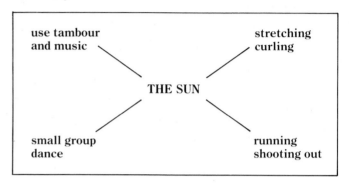

200 Water

whirling splashing up rocking

'Whirl' and 'toss' are developed more fully than 'run' and 'rock'. Help the children link actions together. The use of real water produces vivid quality in the movement. (*See also Ocean pp. 137-143.*)

Questions and tasks

1 Look at the water in the bowl. It's very still. Stretch your hands in front of you (palms down) and make your hands still like the surface of the water. Move them a little and then still again.
2 Watch what I make the water do. I'm making a whirlpool. Find a space. Show me a whirlpool movement. Ready . . . and stop very still.
3 Let's practise some of the ways you found . . . Turn on two feet, stretching out the arms wide.
4 Now whirl the arms upwards and downwards. Sometimes one arm, sometimes two. Make your whole body join in the movement.

5 Try whirling on your bottom. Can you keep your legs up? And then jump up and hop, whirl on one leg. And stop.

6 Turn very slowly, getting lower and lower until you are sitting.

7 Now watch the water. What is it doing? Splashing up and coming down.

8 Let's do that with our hands. Yes, it's a *sudden*, movement up into the air.

9 Standing, listen to the tambourine. Make sudden, splashing jumps into the air.

10 Now use hands or feet 'splashing' upwards.

11 Good, I saw one girl there toss her arms into the air, then turn and jump with her knees in the air.

12 Listen to the sound. When I smooth and rub the tambourine, I want you to dance — whirlpool. When I shake and hit the tambourine change to tossing and leaping.

13 Come close to me now and sit down, not touching, so that you have space to move a little. Watch the water *rocking*.

14 Everyone rock like the water and then stop very still.

The dance

An individual dance
Begin near the teacher. Run and pause, run and pause in the free space of the hall. Choose your own space and whirl and toss there. Smoothly return to the teacher. Slowly turn and sit rocking gently to stillness.

A group dance
Use the above ideas. Each group chooses a particular action and moves in turn.

Summary

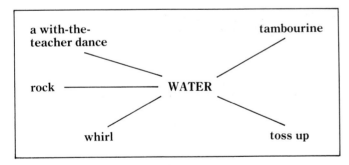

201 Waves

rising,sinking rolling,pressing

Stress variations of these 'pair actions'. Give clear voice rhythms. Stress movement flow. The movement could be linked to a story of a tidal wave. A large piece of fabric might simulate a wave. Two children move it. The others rise and sink, copying the movement. (*See also* **Ocean**, *pp. 137-143*.)

Questions and tasks

1 Rise up high like the wave does, and then sink downwards and rise up again. Lead with your *hands*.

2 Try that group by group. Stretch really high. Lift your arms and legs.

3 See if you can fall bit by bit. Let your head go, your arms, shoulders, back, knees, so that you crumple downwards. Show me your falls, like waves breaking.

4 Group by group once again, rising, falling and rising. See if you can make a wave rhythm. Keep the movement going. Work on your *sequences*.

5 What do people do in the surf? Roll and press upwards to the surface again.

6 Imagine now the surf rolls you over. Ready. Roll and stop. And again. Roll in the surf.

7 I saw a roll and a kick upwards, a slow roll on to the knees with the arms floating up. Let's practise those ways. Roll and kick, and roll and kick.

8 Make it clear how you rolled over; how you press upwards to the surface again. (Pick out sequences. Encourage practising.)

The dance

A short dance of action and reaction arranged by the teacher. Either half the class rises and falls and rises like a huge wave while half the class rolls and presses upwards, or a partner dance.

Summary

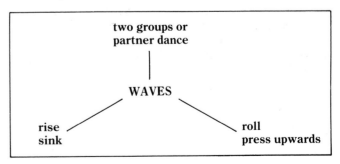

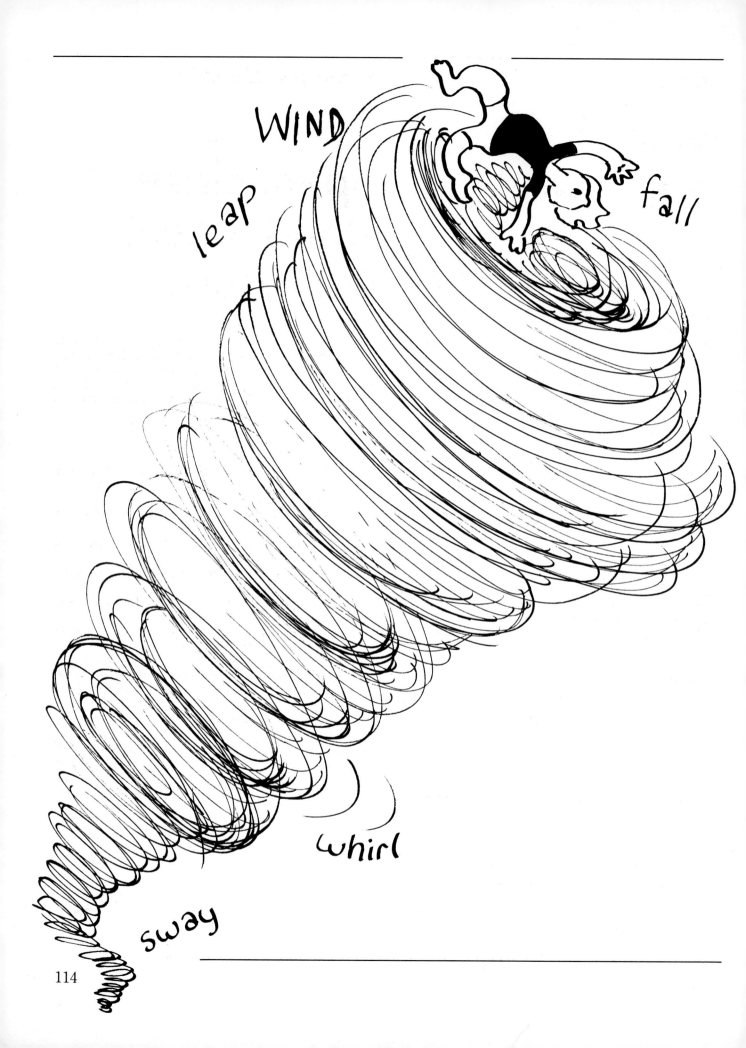

WIND

leap

fall

whirl

sway

whirl, fall leap, sway

203 Angels

open, close stand, kneel walk, turn

The dance is about the movement of people in the wind. Discuss 'wind' with the children. 'What does the wind do to you? How do you feel?'

Here the actions selected are very simple and the creativity lies in the making of simple sequences. Children quickly respond to the idea of linking actions together. It is particularly important to stress the full enactment of each action, such as the sensation of growing and stretching in the 'opening' action.

Accompaniment a slow-pace carol or Indian bells.

Questions and tasks

1 Imagine you're caught in a whirlwind. Try *whirling* and *stopping* very firmly. Do that three times, alternate sides. Each time, open the arms wide as you whirl.
2 Now leap wide in the air as if the wind were tossing you high. Make it clear what the arms and legs do in the air.
3 Let's see half the class at a time now, *linking whirling* with *leaping*. (A short practice, pick out some good sequences.)
4 The wind blows you over. Try *falling, rolling* and *leaping* up again. Pause. Try from different starting positions.
5 A group at a time: run and *leap* in the wind. And run and leap.
6 Everyone begin kneeling, *swaying* the arms from side to side. Make it bigger. Sway until you are standing. Swing in the wind with big movements, rock from side to side.

Questions and Tasks

1 What do angels look like? They have their *arms stretched* out open wide; sometimes they're standing, sometimes kneeling.
2 Move your arms slowly to the sound of the Indian bell. Gently open and close them.
3 Now kneel down slowly as you close them and stand slowly as you open them.
4 Try a *slow turn* with your arms stretching out wide. And the other way.
5 Perhaps you could *turn and kneel* and then stand slowly again.
6 Now *walk* forwards very smoothly opening your arms wide and then closing them again gently.
7 Choose which direction you do your angel walks in.
8 Now sometimes kneel, sometimes stand, sometimes walk, sometimes turn. Show me how *you* begin. Have lots of *stillness*.
9 Make it clear what your arms do as you move. Are they *closing*? Are they opening?
10 Find a partner. See if you can work out some angel movements together. Are you both going to do the same movement or are you going to be different?

The dance

In four groups

Each group decides on one of the phrases of movement. They sort out starting positions and relationships towards and away from each other, one after the other, etc., and perform one group after another, keeping a flow from group to group.

Summary

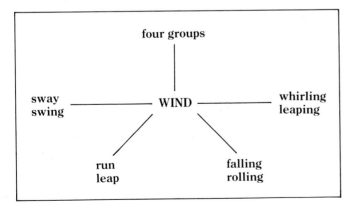

The dance
A partner dance
A kneeling, standing angel; a turning, walking angel. Partners change over. Partners finish in a unison action.
A file dance
A simple follow-my-leader pathway and action, concluding with each angel leaving the file and settling gently in his/her own space.

Summary

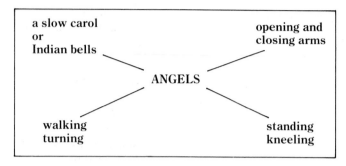

204 Fireworks

shoot up
drift down

It is important to stress 'preparation and recovery', namely how the movement begins and how it ends. Repeat a phrase of movement many times — movement involvement grows with rhythmic repetition. The words could equally well be linked with other images, such as space craft which rocket up and disintegrate downwards. Have a brief discussion about fireworks, linking images to movement, words and sounds. A group of children could play firework percussion.
Accompaniment voice sounds or percussion.

Questions and tasks
1 Everyone jump, shoot your whole self into the air. Lead the movement with the hands. Ready . . . Shoot into the air, and . . .
2 Try now: shoot into the air, land and come down slowly, drift down. Ready . . . Into the air and . . . softly down, down, down. Good, the arms were opening as you moved downwards.
3 What other parts could you shoot upwards? Your head, your knee? This time, vary the part that goes into the air. (Observe and encourage.)

4 All together now, try: run and *knee* jump into the air (many times). Pull the knees right up as you jump.
5 In your new space, practise your sequence of *shoot up* and *drift down*. I'll give you three minutes. I'm going to walk round and see what you are making.
6 Good. (To one child) I liked that low preparation, arms well back. Then you shot into the air with your hands and knee high, landed and did a slow, spiral turn. Do that again many times. Try to control the movement and make it very clear.
7 And sit. How should this dance begin?

The dance
The movement begins from one end of the hall, spreading from one child to the next (like fireworks being let off gradually) until the space is filled with shooting, drifting-down figures. Try a unison ending with everyone making large circles (catherine wheels) with their arms, gradually slowing down to stillness.
Voice sound accompaniment
Half the class accompanies, half moves. For example, use the sound: s h sh sh sh t m m m m m m m (humming).

Summary

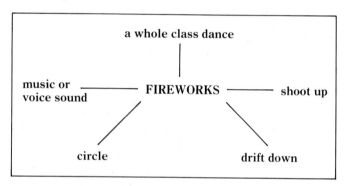

freeze shatter melt

This idea has been used with many different age groups. Adjust the imagery to suit the children. Use it in connection with looking at ice shapes in winter, or experiments with freezing water.
Accompaniment quiet chime bars or Indian bells.

Questions and tasks

1 Icicles? . . . As I point to you, move very slowly into a space and grow into any icicle position. There can be many different shapes. Then melt a little and form a new shape. Keep moving slowly.

2 And come back to me. You have some very good ideas, but let's make them a little clearer. How could you make it better? Yes, you could make the icicles harder, stronger. Show me an icicle *hand*, an icicle *elbow*.

3 Now try the idea (1) again. Remember you can balance on different parts of yourself to make the icicle shape . . .

4 Hold the ice shape now. Imagine I throw a stone and break up the ice, *shatter* the ice. Ready and I THROW . . . Good, that make you really move. What did you *do*?

5 (Answers) You shot your hands into the air? You rolled and balanced? You kicked your toes upward? Let's see some of these. Make it clear what happens to you in movement; what you look like when you stop . . .

6 Everyone try again now. All the movements are sharp and sudden. Try several sharp movements in a row. Ready . . . And *move* and *move* and *move* (fast pace).

7 Now all of you do sharp skips around the room like sharp ice shooting into the air. Use shooting fingers too. Skip and skip and skip and skip and skip and *balance*. Is your knee sharp, your foot pointed?

8 And melt to the ground . . . Melt, melt, melt down into a puddle. And lie very relaxed.

The dance

Two or three of these ideas could be drawn together in a subsequent lesson; for example, the ice forms (individuals or groups of three); the ice breaks and scatters; it melts.
Voice sounds
Humming and sharp sounds (ch, ch, st) could be used by the children as they dance.

Summary

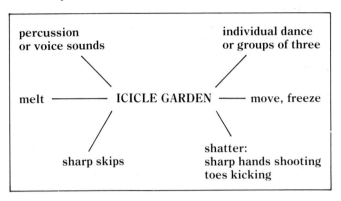

star shapes
bouncing
shooting
disappearing

Make a simple silver star. Use it as a visual stimulus for body shape and movement. This is very useful where there are language problems.
Accompaniment triangle, tambourine.

Questions and tasks

1 Sit near me. Look at the star. Can you make your hand look like that? And the other hand. Now hold up two star hands.
2 Make a star with two hands. Perhaps put your wrists or fingers together. Good. Every time I make a sound on the triangle, you make me star hands . . .
3 Who can move away from me into a *space* and make a *big* star there out of your whole body? Ready . . .

4 Good. Look at those stars. There are some on their knees and some balancing on one leg and . . . (feed in these ideas if necessary).
5 Now lots of times. Keep the movement going. Move and a STAR . . . turn, run, roll into star shapes.
6 Show me your last star shape. Now make your star disappear slowly into the ground. Down, down until you're lying down, limp and still. The stars have gone.
7 Come to crouch position. Now, suddenly there are some *shooting* stars. Ready, jump straight up and shoot your fingers in the air. Do that three times. And . . . shoot and shoot and shoot. *Run* and shoot, and run and shoot and *balance*. Who can balance? A balancing star. And come to me.

The dance
A few of these ideas could be drawn together. Suggest simply: 'Now you make me a star dance. I wonder how you are going to begin.'

Older children have made star dances 'mirroring' star shapes — moving slowly from lying to kneeeling, standing, turning, etc. Give the stars names and use them as part of the dance.

Summary

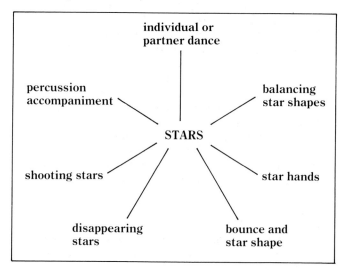

Shapes

207 Cave

stepping lifting crawling

These words stimulate different ways of *travelling* along and group shapes which are made by the children fitting in *over*, *under* and *around* each other. The words are related to the image of a cave.

Questions and tasks
1 Close your eyes. Imagine we are in a cave. Are there rocks, waterfalls, cobwebs? Show me how you move.
2 I saw: stepping over rocks with the *knees* high, lifting the hands over or the feet jumping over; ducking under waterfalls; rolling under ledges; sliding along the ground or backbending under obstacles. Make each movement big and clear. Imagine the cave.
3 Now choose going: *over*, *under* and *around*. Practise some of the movements. Explore the cave. Show me your sequences.
4 See if we can make a rock shape out of bodies. In groups of three. Fit yourselves in close together so one is under, one is over the other. Practise moving slowly into one group shape and then slowly changing it into another.

The dance
Half-the-class dance
Half the children make rock shapes. The other half move around the groups, and move over and under imaginary rocks and, possibly, the 'rock children'.

Summary

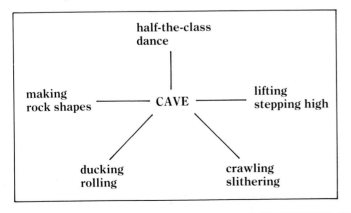

Sound

208 Bounce and Spin

bounce, spin

A beginning lesson for very young children stressing high and low, moving and stopping. Note that spin is not developed as much as bounce.
Follow up with a finger painting using the action of bouncing and spinning fingers.

Questions and tasks
1 Sitting, listen to this bouncy sound on my tambourine. *Bounce* and *bounce* and *bounce*.
2 When the bouncy sound starts I want you to bounce your *fingers* on your knees, and when it stops, *you* stop and be very still. Ready . . . (several times).
3 This time I want you to listen to me as well as the bouncy sound and I will call out which bit of you your hands must bounce on. Like this: bounce your fingers on your knees.
4 As I *point to you* bounce away into a space and sit.
5 Show me your bounces in your space. Here's the bouncing sound . . .
6 Good. I saw some *high*, high ones and some *low* down ones. Show me now when you bounce high and when you bounce low.
7 Good. Some children were opening their arms wide and then closing themselves up tight as they bounced.
8 All sit. Can you put your feet and legs in the *air* in front of you? Stretch them up and bring them down . . . Now who can *spin* on their bottoms with their legs off the ground? Ready, spin . . . Yes, you have to be very strong.
9 Now, stand and look around for another space. Point to that space. And this time: bounce and bounce and bounce and BURST in that new space. Ready . . . Who can stop very still? Are you all in terrible burst positions? Look how he's landed! And again: bounce and bounce and bounce and BURST.

The dance

An individual dance

A 'bounce and burst' dance, which is just a repetition of 9, with the added directive of: 'Show me how you begin and how you end. I wonder what sort of bounce *you* are going to do.' Use music. Fade it for the last 'burst'.

Summary

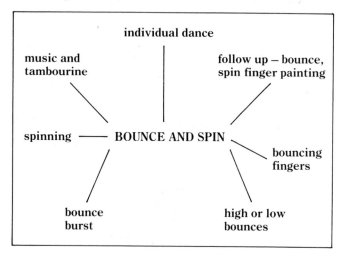

individual dance

music and tambourine

follow up – bounce, spin finger painting

spinning —— BOUNCE AND SPIN

bouncing fingers

bounce burst

high or low bounces

209 Drum-Beat

stamp
jump
shrug
beat

Contrast *feet* movement with *shoulder* and *hand* or *fist* movement. Encourage older children to produce a definite *step pattern* through putting together steps, jumps, hops with the music.

Accompaniment drumming.

Follow up making drum-beat rhythms; beating out *their* movement pattern; combining their 'tune' with another's; tape recording the rhythms.

Questions and tasks

1 What can your *feet* do to the music? Jumps? Show me. Everyone practise.
2 Everyone try this one: stamp, stamp, step — hop; stamp, stamp, step — hop.
3 Or *jump* the feet: across and apart; across and apart; or side to side; forwards and backwards.
4 Try that sideways jump. Feet together. And bounce and bounce and a run-run jump. Make it go with the music.
5 Make *groups of three*. See if you can work out together a jumping, stepping pattern of movement. I will go round and help you.
6 Now make some *shoulder* movements, shrugging, or fist-beating movements: shrug and shrug and a beat, beat, beat. Make the movements large. Make the whole body join in.
7 Stand well spaced out, facing each other in threes. You are going to dance *one* at a time. The *first* one dances around the other *two* and back to place, and so on. The two who are not dancing around can use shoulder or fist movements on the spot.

The dance

In threes

Each group works out a stepping, jumping pattern and decides *when* and *where* they shall move in relationship to each other. (Forwards and away, in and out, all together etc.) The dance might end with groups meeting and mingling in the centre of the room.

Younger children enjoy making freer variations of stepping, jumping, stamping, hopping, with perhaps a simple *unison* step near the teacher to begin and end the dance.

Summary

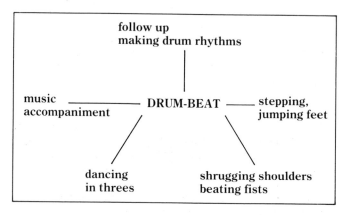

follow up making drum rhythms

music accompaniment —— DRUM-BEAT —— stepping, jumping feet

dancing in threes

shrugging shoulders beating fists

210 Feet Talk

Make up a *foot chant* or use names, nursery rhymes etc. for the feet to dance to.

jump, hop stride, shake kick, turn

Dances based on *feet* can lead to a wide variety of styles and moods. They can be dramatic or highly rhythmic.
Follow up drawing different kinds of feet and then dancing the ideas, or draw round everyone's feet on one huge sheet of paper. Add words and thoughts.

Questions and tasks

1 *Shake* your feet. *Stamp* your feet. *Jump* your feet. *Run* your feet and stop. Really get your feet moving.
2 Here's a jumping rhythm (or sound). Show me jumping and stopping. Perhaps jump your feet apart and then together. Really stretch them in the air, turn as you jump.
3 Practise hopping on one foot, then the other. What does the leg in the air do? Practise these ideas to the rhythm.
4 Rub your feet with your hands. Have a good look at them.
5 Now stretch both legs up into the air. Try some 'feet talk' in the air with your feet, ankles and toes.
6 Let's use the *foot chant* now for striding and jumping. Say it and do it with me: left foot right foot; left foot right foot; feet feet feet. Work out a hopping, skipping, jumping pattern.

The dance

1 *Individual choice* of movement with the woodblock as accompaniment, alternating with a class *unison action* using the chant as the accompaniment: dancing in your own space around the teacher; moving towards her on the chant.
2 *Very young children* enjoy the rhythmic enactment of simple action words: 'my striding feet'; 'my jumping feet' etc.
3 *Older children* like making jumping, turning, skipping sequences which can be as complex as their skills allow. Use fast-pace rhythmic music.

Summary

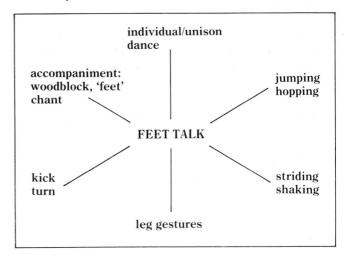

individual/unison dance

accompaniment: woodblock, 'feet' chant

jumping hopping

FEET TALK

kick turn

striding shaking

leg gestures

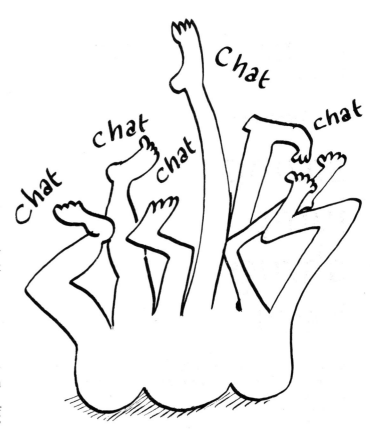

chat chat chat chat

211 Magic Sound

bounce
skip
clap

Summary

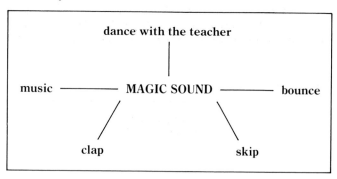

This is for a class of young children with very little movement experience. Stress body awareness and 'space words'; 'away from', 'back to', 'high'. The aim is to communicate some basic ways of moving and stimulate an interest in different ways of moving.
Accompaniment use a tambourine to begin with, then music.
Follow up look at pictures of animals or moving things. What do they do? Do the movements with arms and hands as they sit. Make collections of movement pictures.

Questions and tasks

1 All sit near me and bounce your fists on the floor just as though your fists were like rubber balls: bounce and bounce and bounce and bounce and stop. And higher bounces . . .
2 Now, one by one as I call your name, run and find your space on the floor and sit there. It mustn't be near a wall. You must have a space all round you. Ready . . .
3 Now everyone has a space, so everyone bounces on the spot. Come on, bounce . . . They were marvellous bounces. I saw some knees high, heads high. Try again and this time, as the bouncy sound gets very *quiet*, I want you to bounce back to me.
4 I wonder who could find their space again? Listen this time to the skipping sound (tambour) and skip to your space . . . And skip back to me.
5 Sit near me and listen to the music. You all sit like statues. When the music begins, you come alive and clap and bounce your hands to the music. Good, clapping high and clapping low.
6 Let's make a dance now. Stand like statues near me. When the music begins it brings you alive. You *skip* away to your own space, then make a *bouncing, clapping* dance on your own space. As the music gets quieter, you skip back to me and turn into a statue again.

The dance
With the teacher
Many infant dances can follow this plan: starting near, travelling into the space and returning. Different actions could obviously be used.

212 Messages with Sound

clicking
stamping
slapping

Experiment with making sounds through clicking the fingers, stamping the floor, slapping the body, etc. Make sequences of sounds. Spend time exploring these. These can be sound 'messages'. Develop high and low so the body is fully involved.

Questions and tasks

1 Everyone listen hard. I am going to send you a *message* with my feet. You send the same message back: (teacher) Stamp, stamp — stamp — stamp; (children) Stamp, stamp — stamp — stamp.
2 Try some more sounds now. You find them. *Clicking* fingers high and low and all around the body: *clapping* and leaping; *stamping* forwards and backwards; *slapping* rhythms on the body — slap the side, the feet, the hands; slap the side, the feet, the hands.
3 Everyone now make up your own message. You can make clicking, slapping, stamping sounds and movement. Use high and low. Move the whole body.
4 Find a partner. Send your partner a message. 'Talk' to each other with sounds and movement. Sometimes say the same thing, sometimes different.
5 Good. Try not to 'talk' at the same time. Listen to and watch your partner, then move and sound. Move one after the other.
6 I will choose some children who are sending really clear messages.

The dance

A partner dance using contrasting sequences of body-part action. The expression may become either witty or angry. Encourage copying the message or sending back a *different* one.

Summary

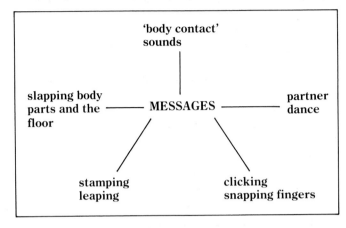

213 Names

stepping turning circling

Aim for variety of movement through moving to the *rhythm* of the child's name. Give several examples and encourage full enactment of the movement to the rhythm. Action to a specific rhythm needs to be repeated many times.

Questions and tasks

1 Sit near me. All say and clap Angela's name together: Angela Viber, Angela Viber.
2 Everyone in a space. Ready, say and move the name: Angela Viber, *Ange*la Viber, stepping and *jump*ing, stepping and *jump*ing. Try it lots of times. Make it clear when you step, when you jump.
3 Good, look at those *arms*. They swing across and *open* to accent the jump. Everyone show me four times now with the rhythm . . .
4 Now, quickly form a circle. I'll point to someone. We'll all say her name lots of times. Then we'll say it and dance it. You choose how you move. You can jump it, stamp it, turn it. Use high and low. Keep on saying and moving. Keep it going. Ready . . . Harpreet *Gup*ta, Harpreet *Gup*ta.

5 Good. I can see different movements with heads and *fingers*. Harpreet Gupta . . .
6 Now a very quiet one. Whisper it, travel to another space. Derek Joseph, Derek Joseph . . . . and *stop*.
7 Everyone sit near me. Let's all say: Sangeeta Ahluwalia — a beautiful *long* name. Make big smooth circles with arms and head. Ready . . .

The dance

Many ideas might evolve, including perhaps an individual idea leading to a unison dance.
1 The children begin moving, whispering and dancing their own name. Stress body parts. The sound increases, the movement gets larger.
2 A sudden stop.
3 They all dance around one child, chanting his name. (Think of an ending.)

Summary

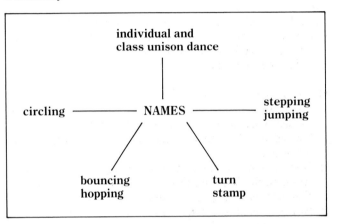

214 Percussion Dance

shaking hitting

The instrument is used to encourage moving high and low and around with a partner. Younger children can play alone or with the teacher. For preference use home-made shakers, small enough to handle easily. Preparatory classroom work in picking up, putting down, shaking it and holding it still, is useful.

Questions and tasks

1 Half the class sits near me. The other half finds a space. Stand with your shakers stretched high above your head.
2 Now *shake* it and hit it high and low. Ready . . . three times . . . You must really *stretch* as high as you can and *bend* your knees to play it low. (Change over groups.)

3 This group plays it so high in the air that you have to jump or skip . . . Play it on the spot. (Change over groups.)

4 This group does eight skips to another space as you play the shaker. Start *low*, end high on your toes. Ready . . . And one and two and three (etc.). And again. This time *turn* as you play . . . (Change groups.)

5 Everyone in a space. Reach out with your shaker *far* from your body. Now play it around the body in big circles. Yes, over your head and round and up high and behind you. Really stretch your body into the space.

6 Try changing over hands as you play. Hold the shaker in one hand, then the other.

The dance
A partner dance
Make a shaker dance together. Do you stay on the same spot or do you travel around your partner with the shaker? Use high and low.

Summary

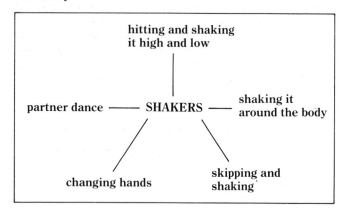

215 Sausages, Chips and Ice-cream

twist
shoot
glide

Choose from the *children's* favourite foods or drinks to make 'food rhythms'. Note the repetition to evolve movement rhythms. Use contrasting movement to express the words. Experiment with different ways of *saying* and *moving*.
Follow up tape-record a chant, or play the rhythm on percussion instruments. Discuss 'What do we think about the food we eat?'

Questions and tasks

1 What's your favourite food? Sausages, chips and ice-cream. How should we say 'sausages'? Slowly, softly.

2 Move your arms softly and slowly, twisting and turning them up and down. Say 'sausages' gently as you move.

3 Now move your backs, bending and stretching, moving up and down. Use your shoulders too.

4 Say 'chips' very sharply. As you say 'chips', shoot up into the air. Repeat the word 'chips'. Show me your jump to 'chips'.

5 I saw a shooting jump with the feet together followed by a hop, then a turning jump. Let's all try that: chips, chips, chips; jump, hop and turning jump.

6 Find a partner. One say and move 'sausages', then the other say and move 'chips'. Think of a starting position. All the 'sausages', ready . . . All the 'chips', ready . . .

7 Everyone gather near me. Let's say 'ice-cream' very smoothly. Repeat it lots of times.

8 Now stretch out your arms and hands and do a big, smooth, gliding turn as you say 'ice-cream'.

9 Say and move 'ice-cream' several times. Do you finish high or low?

10 Try gliding round now with another part of you leading the movement. Perhaps your elbows or one foot. Keep it very smooth.

11 Now choose whether you like sausages, chips or ice-cream movement best. When I hold up the word 'sausages', only the 'sausage' people move. Keep on repeating the word. Show me your movement ideas. Repeat with 'chips' and 'ice-cream'.

12 Now all say and do your food at the same time.

The dance
Near the teacher
Everyone chanting quietly, 'sausages, chips and ice-cream'. At a signal from the teacher they whisper their way to their own space. The children have already decided who is going to say 'sausages', who 'chips', who 'ice-cream'. They choose a starting position which could relate to the shape of the food they are chanting. All the 'sausages' say and move, perhaps four times, and freeze; then the 'chips' move; and then the 'ice-cream'. To end, all simultaneously say their food loudly, becoming softer, and finish near the floor.

Older children could work in twos or threes, sharing the words and the movement between them.

Summary

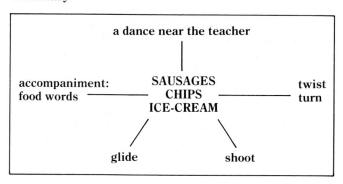

Poetry and Story

216 'Fog'

> The fog comes
> on little cat feet,
> it sits looking
> over harbour and city
> on silent haunches
> and then moves on.

This poem by Carl Sandburg comes from *Wordscapes* by Barry Maybury (Oxford University Press).

spreading
tiptoeing
swirling

The poem is a starting image for ideas arising from 'fog'. The main quality in the lesson is lightness. Therefore, have a vigorous warm-up. Note the movement contrasts. Make sure that the body is fully extended. Give rhythms, especially in 3, for practising the movements.
Accompaniment use the action words to encourage qualitative movement.

Questions and tasks

1 Close your eyes while I read the poem. Can you see the picture in your mind? What does it look like (etc.)? 'It's very white and soft,' says one child. 'It moves slowly.'
2 Sit by me and put your fingers together very gently, hardly touching. Now move them apart into the space as if you are making the fog, spreading the fog all around you with your hands and fingers (very gently opening and closing the arms).
3 Can you tiptoe 'on little cat feet' into a space of your own? . . . Now stretch up and out on tiptoe. Then make the fog all around you with your fingertips. Make it high, make it to the side (etc.).
4 Stretch up high and wide . . .
Tiptoe into another space and make the fog in the new space.
5 Now half of you are going to be quite still in your space anywhere on the floor. You choose whether you are kneeling, or curled on your side, or stretching high . . .

6 The other half spread out in the spaces between them . . . You are going to move among them, spreading fog. This time the fog moves *fast, swirling* and stretching and changing direction . . . Then listen to the cymbal. Slow down and stop with the sound.
7 There were some lovely movements there. Some people were really stretching high and opening their arms far away from their bodies, and then closing down low.
8 Change places and let's see if the second group can listen to the cymbal as it makes you go faster and slower. The ones who aren't spreading fog? . . . Yes, you could be like people moving very slowly in the fog. Can you try moving slowly from standing, to kneeling, to sitting as the fog swirls around you? Ready . . .
9 Can everyone practise that swirling turn? Look how he starts with his arms stretched high and then dips them down to one side, turns and opens them high. Everyone try . . .
10 How shall we make our fog dance?

The dance

The fog comes from everywhere. The children crouch at the sides of the room. They gradually move — first of all tiptoeing, then swirling with faster and larger movements. As the cymbal stops, they freeze their position. The teacher moves amongst them, touching them gently, and they gently sink to a lying positon. The fog has gone.

Summary

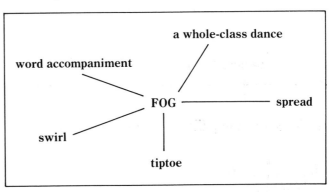

125

217 Humbug

(to be said when grumpy)

> HUMBUG
> BUGBEAR
> BUGABOO
> BUGBANE
> LADYBUG
> BODYBUG
> BUGSEED

From *Bugwords* by Alastair Reid from *Junior Voices, Book 3.*

grip
swing
stamp, leap

The action words chosen are arbitrary. Relate the words to *body-part* movement. 'Humbug' is a strong, angry word which goes with strong, angry movement sequences. Say it fast, say it slowly. (*See 16 and 89.*)

Questions and tasks

1 All sit by me. Say 'Humbug' with me loudly and clearly. Ready . . . And again . . .
2 As you say it, *grip* your fists tightly. Ready . . . 'Humbug!' Now say it inside your head, but still make the movement *strong*.
3 Find yourself a space on the floor and take up any strong position, standing — fists clenched — legs strong.
4 Now swing your arm and clench your fist as you say 'Humbug!' What position are you in? There's a fierce one.
5 Say it many time now. Make the swings really large. Use your whole body.
6 Good, some people took their swing from high to low, bending their backs. Someone turned his. All try that. Ready . . . Say and move 'Humbug!' lots of times.
7 Find a partner. Face your partner in a stong position.
8 This time, open wide and then do an enormous leap as you say 'Humbug!' Both together — Ready: 'Humbug!'
9 Now move one after the other. Finish high or low.
10 Make your dance with your partner. Move and say 'Humbug'. Make it fierce with big movements. Show me how you begin — how you end. Use sequences of movement. Find some more big, strong movements and body shapes.

11 Good. Two boys here are using: open and leap, swing and fists. They are using the same movement. Another two are: swinging down into a roll and a leap, leaping using fists. That was a new idea.
12 Everyone quite still. Show me your dance . . . Finish quite still.
13 Everyone quietly back to me. Listen to these words: HUMBUG, BUGBANE, LADYBUG, BODYBUG, BUGSEED.
14 All say them . . . All whisper them . . . Now each of you choose one. Now all say your word loudly at the same time. Ready . . .

The dance

1 A partner dance based on one word.
2 A partner dance based on two words.
3 A class dance — everyone sounds and moves his word one by one. Then all sound together many times, moving vigorously. At a signal, they whisper their word and return to a sitting position.

The next lesson could develop this content into a richer assortment of strong movement, or more practice of observed actions.

Other words, angrily spoken, could be alternative accompaniment — names of things they dislike, perhaps.

Summary

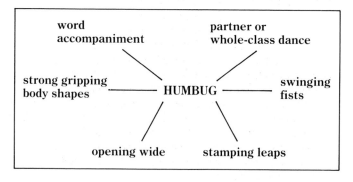

218 'The Rain Dance'

The fire flickered with a flare,
The ghostly figure *leapt in the air.*
Huge shadows fell across the ground
When the figure landed without any sound.
A piercing scream, a bongo beat,
A tossing head, two stamping feet.
Legs bent at knees, feet wide apart,
A twisting body, a thudding heart.
The drums beat out, loud and clear
D-rr-um-dum-dum, the time draws near.
The *twirling* body leaps again
Trying hard to make it rain.

The Rain Dance by Marina Brunskill from *Wordscapes* by Barry Maybury (Oxford University Press).

Use these words as a basis for action phrases. Some children could clap and chant the words while others dance. Emphasize the landing in the jump.

leap, land
toss, stamp

Questions and tasks

1 Stand still and straight. Bounce very gently. Feel the floor with your feet, very easy, no sound on landing. And still. Remember it's all very quiet.
2 Now I want you to do a large jump on the spot and land very gently. It's like a cat jump — very careful. Ready and . . . JUMP!
3 Good. Can you see how it makes the ending of your jump — your position — very important? Now try a jump from two feet landing on one. Ready, with the rhythm, four of those jumps and soft, soft landings . . . Legs bent at knees, feet wide apart. Anywhere round the room, huge jumps and soft landings.
4 Everyone join in as I say the words:
   'The fire flickered with a flare,
   The ghostly figure leapt in the air.
   Huge shadows fell across the ground
   When the figure landed without any sound.'
5 Half of you sit in a circle — you are going to chant and clap to the words. Half of you stand inside the circle — you are going to practise: leap and land. This is in the darkness around a fire. I'll beat the drum too. (The centre group practise 'leap and land' as the circle claps and chants.) Ready. Come on now, up on your toes, open your arms, prepare to leap and . . . (chant).
6 Change over groups.
7 Try the same idea with 'toss and stamp'. Chant and clap: 'A tossing head, two stamping feet.'

The dance

A circle dance with an inner and outer group contrasting activities. Quiet clapping from the circle. Inner group begin (one after another) leaping and landing until they are all leaping. A sudden stop. Inner group sit and begin clapping the toss, stamp rhythm. The other group circle around them tossing and stamping.

Devise an ending. Perhaps everyone sinks down, spread-eagled on the ground, waiting for the rain. Other sounds could supplement the clapping, e.g. drum-beats, tapping the floor.

Summary

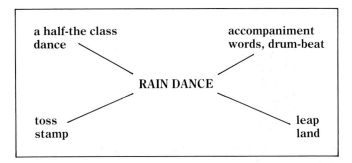

219 'The Wandering Moon'

Age after age and all alone,
   She turns through endless space,
Showing the watchers on the earth
   Her round and rocky face.
Enchantment comes upon all hearts
   That feel her lonely grace.

Mount Newton is the highest peak
   Upon the wandering moon,
And there perhaps the witches dance
   To some fantastic tune,
And in the half-light cold and grey
   Their incantations croon.

And there perhaps mad creatures come
   To play at hide-and-seek
With howling apes and blundering bears
   And bats that swoop and squeak.
I cannot see what nameless things
   Go on at Newton Peak.

I cannot tell what vessels move
   Across the Nubian Sea,
Nor whether any bird alights
   On any stony tree.
A quarter of a million miles
   Divide the moon and me.

A quarter of a million miles —
   It is a fearsome way,
But ah! if we could only fly
   On some auspicious day
And land at last on Newton Peak,
   And then, what games we'd play!

What songs we'd sing on Newton Peak,
   On what wild journeys go
By frozen fen or burning waste,
   Or where the moon-flowers grow,
And countless strange and fearful things —
   If only we could know!

The Wandering Moon by James Reeves from *Complete Poems for Children* (Heinemann).

turn, circle
run, stop
twist
grow, shrivel

Introduce the poem before the dance lesson. Choose one image from each verse.
Accompaniment background percussion sounds. Children could make up the accompaniment.

Questions and tasks
1 Think of the shape of the moon. Draw a huge, moon-shaped circle in front of the body with your right arm. Stretch high over to the side, down to the floor and back. Bend and stretch your legs.
2 Try stretching and circling one arm, then the other and *turn* slowly and smoothly.
3 All sit by me. Remember that we decided that the 'mad creatures' move fast and stop in weird shapes. (Still sitting.) First, practise moving your *hands* fast in every direction. Move the hands suddenly high, suddenly sideways (etc.).
4 Find a space. Listen to the woodblock. Practise short runs and stops in mad shapes. Use different directions.
5 There's a good one. He stopped with his head near the ground, hand and one heel in the air. Everyone practise, run and stop, with a part of you high in the air.

The dance
The words: twisting (witches) and strange growing (moon-flowers) could be similarly explored. Make a dance in *four groups* based on: moon; witch; mad creatures; moon-flower; each with a different percussion accompaniment.

One class devised a unison ending to the dance. All the children joined the 'moon-flower' group, then 'grew' into an enormous moon-flower. The moon-flower shrivelled and collapsed.

Summary

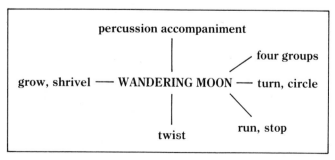

percussion accompaniment

grow, shrivel — WANDERING MOON — turn, circle

four groups

twist

run, stop

dodge
creep

Although 'dodge' and 'creep' are the initial actions, others (like rolling, leaping, slithering) will be added as the movement is developed. Emphasize the main contrast between moving fast and slowly.

Use imagery which evolves with the movement. A dramatic effect is achieved if half the children are moving fast and the others slowly, simultaneously.
Accompaniment woodblock — dodging, tambour — creeping.
Follow up writing or tape-recording an adventure story.

Questions and tasks
1 Sit near me. Watch my hands. Wherever they dodge in the space, you copy (up, down, to the side).
2 Standing. Face me and whichever direction I dodge in, you copy. Ready . . . this way, etc.
3 Now listen to the sound of the woodblock. Dodge with the *sound*.
4 Choose which direction you go in. Show me.
5 How fast can you make your feet go? Can you change direction quickly?
6 Listen to the sound of the tambour. Show me slow, slow creeping, close to the ground.
7 Try crawling and creeping, sometimes on your hands and knees, sometimes on your feet.
8 This boy has thought of *slithering*, too. Which part of his body is he moving along on?
9 Everyone practise now — crawling, creeping, slithering. Keep on changing the part of your body you are moving on.
10 Keep it slow and careful.
11 Listen to the accompaniment now. With the *woodblock* you move fast — dodging, turning, moving up and down in different directions. With the *tambour* beat you move slowly and carefully, close to the ground.
12 When the sound stops, you stop — high or low — and listen.
13 Now let's have two groups of children: number one group will move on the dodging sound; number two on the creeping sound.

The dance

The class decides where the movement could be taking place (i.e. a location — a jungle, a haunted house) and the action sequence is arranged accordingly.

We think we are being pursued. We creep and dodge and listen, then run to safety to the centre of the room.

Summary

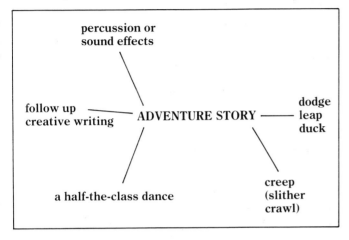

```
              percussion or
              sound effects
                    \
                     \
follow up             \
creative writing ——— ADVENTURE STORY ——— dodge
                     /                     leap
                    /                      duck
                   /
                  /              creep
a half-the-class dance          (slither
                                 crawl)
```

221 Shaky King

This is a story of a king who could not stop shaking. His people thought of many *action* cures. Finally, one *did* cure him.

Use *shaking* combined with other actions. Think of 'cures' which use contrasting body parts or qualities. Make a paper-bag puppet of the king. Alternate the puppet shaking with the people moving a 'cure'.
Follow up making king paper-bag puppets.

Questions and tasks

1 Listen to the shaking sound. Show me how the king can't stop shaking . . .
2 Everyone do shaky runs, and shaky jumps, and shaky falling down, and shake all over, and STOP.
3 Sit by me. Let's think of a magic movement to cure the king. Five claps and a stamp? Ready . . . clap, clap, clap, clap, clap, STAMP. Galloping on a fast horse? Ready . . . and STOP. Swimming in cold water? Show me . . . and STOP. Turning round ten times? Swinging his arms? (etc.)
4 Here's the king (the paper-bag puppet). He is shaking and shaking. I am going to play some music now and you are going to dance your 'cures' for the king to see if you can stop him shaking. Here's the music. Which movements shall we begin with? A jumping, jumping, jumping cure.
5 And he's still shaking. So dance another cure.

The dance

A teacher (puppet) and class dance
The puppet shakes and stops. The children dance a 'cure'. The puppet shakes, etc. . . . until one cure does stop him.

Alternatively, the children can be kings, can shake and stop in a variety of shaky shapes, while a 'people' paper-bag puppet jumps or whirls to cure them. While the puppet moves, the children must be still and vice versa.

Summary

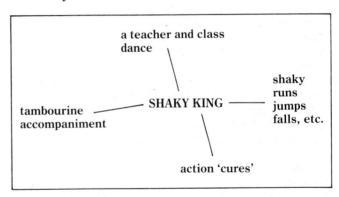

```
              a teacher and class
              dance
                    \
                     \                      shaky
                      \                     runs
tambourine             \                    jumps
accompaniment ——— SHAKY KING ———            falls, etc.
                      /
                     /
                    /
              action 'cures'
```

shake

stamp
wriggle
creep

The story in brief

In 'Stamping Elephant' by Anita Hewett in *Tell Me Another Story* (Puffin), Elephant will not stop stamping. Various forest creatures try to cure him. Mouse finally does so by creeping into his trunk while he is asleep and refusing to go until he promises to behave. There are many possible variations of the above idea. Most important is to abstract a *few* movement ideas, so that it is the flow and variety of the *movement* that is paramount, rather than miming the story.

The elephant, the snake or the mouse could each form the basis of a separate lesson. The next lesson might develop the sinuous wriggling movement to a suitable piece of music.

Questions and tasks

 1 Who remembers Elephant? What did he DO?
 2 Stay near me. All together, three stamps. Stamp, stamp, stamp!
 3 Can you finish in a strong shape — strong arms, strong legs?
 4 One boy was beating his fists as he stamped. All try that.
 5 Ready — creep into your space.
 6 Listen to the rhythm on the tambour. Show me some big stamps and stop.
 7 Lift your knees and arms high as you stamp. Make yourself large.
 8 Now run fast into another space and stop, and into another space and stop.
 9 Listen to this fast stamping in rhythm on the tambour. Ready — fast stamping.
10 Good. I saw someone stamping and jumping on two feet, and someone else turning and stamping. How many ways can you find?
11 I've brought a snake (a stocking stuffed with foam rubber) to show you. Sit down and watch me move him. Watch how he wriggles and twists on the floor.
12 You try wriggling and twisting, moving as much as you can. Listen to the tambourine. Ready . . . Watch this child rolling and wriggling, using his knees — all try that.
13 Watch how the snake wriggles high and low. You wriggle high and low.

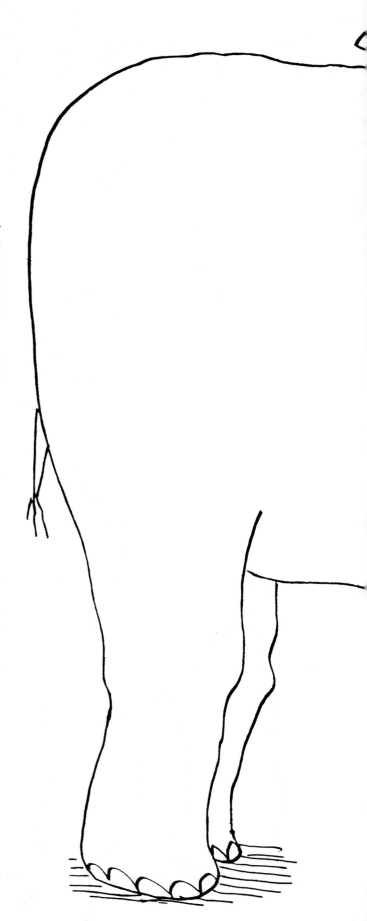

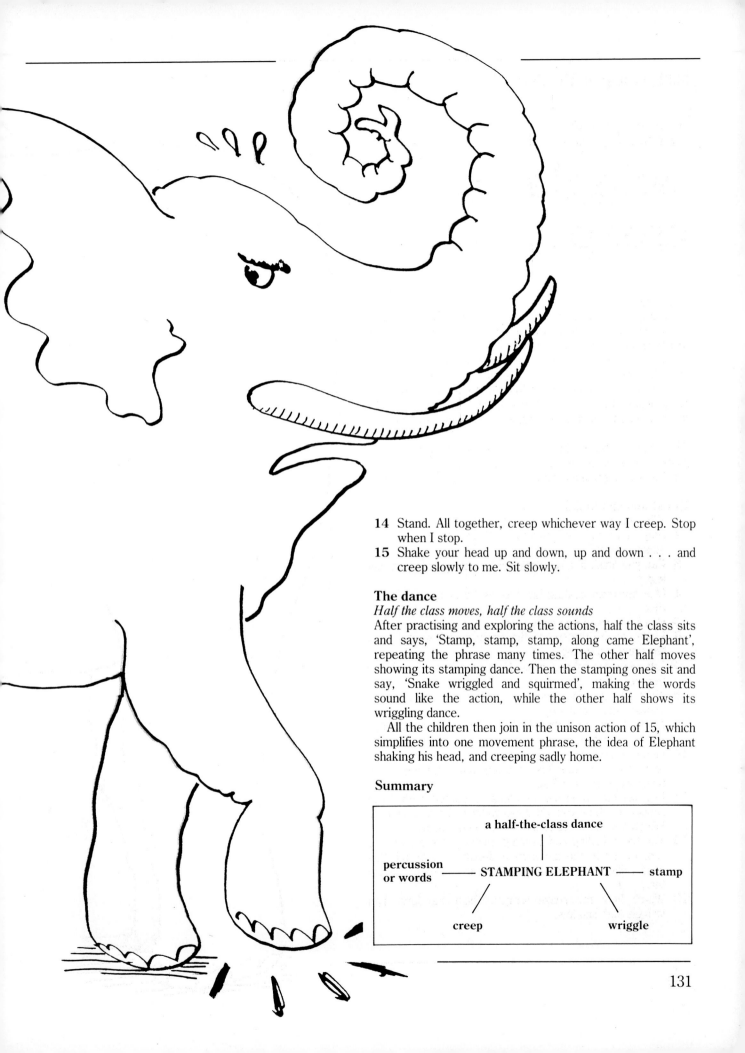

14 Stand. All together, creep whichever way I creep. Stop when I stop.

15 Shake your head up and down, up and down . . . and creep slowly to me. Sit slowly.

The dance
Half the class moves, half the class sounds

After practising and exploring the actions, half the class sits and says, 'Stamp, stamp, stamp, along came Elephant', repeating the phrase many times. The other half moves showing its stamping dance. Then the stamping ones sit and say, 'Snake wriggled and squirmed', making the words sound like the action, while the other half shows its wriggling dance.

All the children then join in the unison action of 15, which simplifies into one movement phrase, the idea of Elephant shaking his head, and creeping sadly home.

Summary

```
                              a half-the-class dance
                                       |
percussion
or words    —    STAMPING ELEPHANT    ——    stamp
                        /        \
                  creep            wriggle
```

Pictures

223 Hands

Photographs might be used as a stimulus

open, close dart, press

Explore slow-motion hand movements and quick-pace ones. Use imagery to help develop the movement. Use 'mirroring' partner work. Choose a vigorous starting activity.
Follow up handprints (using paint) made by different *parts* of the hands, or hand poems.

Questions and tasks

1 Sit near me. All together in slow motion: open your hands, close them, twist them. Now rub them together. Smooth over the backs of the hands. Massage your palms with your thumbs. Pull and stroke down your fingers. Really look at your hands.
2 Watch your hands. As they open, stretch them far away from you. Stretch the whole body. As they close, close up the whole body. Curl in.
3 With a partner: one leads the movement, one copies — like seeing yourself in a mirror. Move your hands in the space, like hands in a dream. See what movements your hands lead you into. Pause and let me see what your hands look like.
4 Try now fast, agitated hands — hands which dash and dart all around the body like fast insects.
5 Now move around the room moving your hands *high* and *low* in any way you choose. I will pick out some interesting ways for everyone to practise. Good — moving with twisting wrists, wriggling fingers, pressing the palms up and down.

The dance

A 'hand dance' with a partner. Titles might arise, such as, 'fierce', 'tired' or 'sad' hands. Try moving sometimes with the hands in contact, finger tips or wrists touching.

Summary

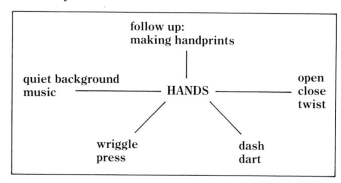

132

Colourful Locations

224 Mars

walking

'Walking' is a starting point for fantasy. Walking becomes 'getting along'. All kinds of strange travelling can be experimented with, but note that *size, extension* and making *rhythmic sequences* are stressed throughout. Avoid restricted movements — work for flow. Have a brief preparatory discussion near the beginning of the lesson about how people or creatures might move on Mars. In this lesson, children's suggestions are starting points. With less experienced children, the latter might equally well be the teacher's examples.

Questions and tasks

1 'Slowly' is the word I want you to think about. Now, as I point to you, one by one, I want you to walk any way you like *slowly* into a space and stay there very still in any position you think is right for Mars . . . Listen to the music. Ready . . .
2 People walked in some very strange ways then. Let's all practise some of them.
3 Try walking high with the fingertips leading you high, really stretched up, then curling down to the ground and up again: High, high and *high* and down, down, down, and high . . . Good, some people were curling down into a tight, twisted shape, really opening themsleves out high and coming right down. Try that again, lots of times.
4 That was a weird one. You were thinking of a green foot? Everyone try his *foot-high-in-the-air* step.
5 Now try these big, floppy walks and slide to the ground: And walk and walk and slide the hands down, And walk . . . as if you have no bones. Yes, make the heads and arms flop as you walk.
6 Lie on the floor very relaxed and still. Breathe, don't move but when I tap the tambour imagine your movement begins. You move in the silence. When I tap again, your movement ends.
7 We have had some really weird walks. Now, with a *partner*, practise a phrase of getting along. Try to move in contact so you are joined together. Begin and end together in a still position. Ready, I give you a tap on the tambour for your movement beginning. A tap for ending. You move in the silence between the taps. That's how long you have.

The dance

A partner dance can develop from 7. The children can work out a movement sequence and decide where they will dance in relationship to each other. How does their dance end? Think of an action word ending. For example, disappear, disintegrate, explode!

The following extract from children's poems show how this dance stimulated writing, phrases from which were used in the next lesson as both movement stimulus and vocal accompaniment:

> Floppy and gooey and
> Shiny with gold
> He goes along upon
> His nose.

Tina (8 years)

Summary

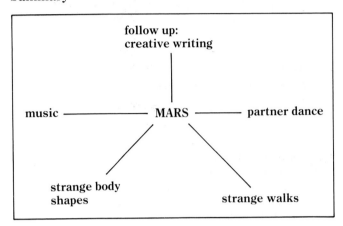

225 Swimming Pool

float
open, close
dive

Many other actions could be used. It is important to choose a *few* contrasting ideas and deeply explore the sensation of the movement so that it becomes a body rhythm. Note that one idea (2-4) is directed and used to extend the body. The other idea (5) gives opportunity for creativity.

Questions and tasks

1 Stand very still in your space. Close your eyes. Imagine floating in warm water. Move gently. The water is so buoyant it holds you up. Floating . . . floating . . . and rest. Some people were moving their elbows, heads, fingers really gently, lightly.
2 Now *swim* in the water. Show me breast-stroke arms. Ready? The hands push upwards, *open* wide and close in downwards; push up, open and close in.

3 As you push, stretch up as high as you can. As you open, arch the back, be as wide as you can. Make the whole body join in the movement, bend the knees. Keep the movement going. Ready . . .

4 Now step up and down smoothly with breast-stoke arms. Make the movement rise up and sink down. Use your backs.

5 Try it now from a *different position*. See if you can use your legs too. Yes, lie *on your back* and make your legs swim in the air. Bend and open and together . . . and then on to your *knees* and close in . Let's all do that idea.

6 Ready for a diving position (any diving starting position; stimulate variety) . . . and another . . . and another . . . and balance. Can you stay there? There were lots of good ideas then. Hands and one foot on the floor, the other one *stretched* high behind. A ready-to-dive wide standing postion; a dive shape, knee tucked under on the floor.

7 All together, try moving into three different dive shapes: press into a dive shape; press into a dive shape; press into a dive shape.

The dance
A half-the-class dance
Half the class sits in a large circle (symbolizing the pool). Half the class stands in the circle (ready to jump into the water). As the water sound begins, they jump into the 'pool' (into the circle) and make a swimming dance — opening, closing arms, turning, diving downwards, stretching forwards, etc. As the music fades, they return to the edge and hold their position. The groups change over.

A partner dance
Swimming together.

Summary

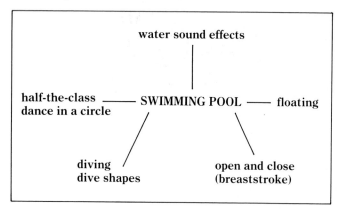

Machines
226 The Machine

stretch out, in
press up, down
swing round
and round
jerk forwards

Follow children's suggestions about what machines 'do'. Perhaps draw a machine and translate it into movement. The above can also be used to encourage awareness of space around the body. Children's voice sounds are the best accompaniment. But do not introduce voice accompaniment until the movement is clear and controlled. Have a vigorous free-flowing warm up.
Accompaniment voice sound or reggae.
Follow up make huge junk machine.

Questions and tasks
1 Sitting near me, not too close to each other, show me with your *hands* the sort of movement your machine does. Yes, everyone try that one: and stretch the hands and grip, and out and *in*, and out and in. Make the movement bigger, make it stronger, come to standing and: out and in — and STILL. That was like a huge grabbing machine.

2 Try another one: (press) *up* and *down* and up and down. Use your *arms* and *hands*. Use your *whole body* (many times). You make your own machine movement now. What sort of a machine is it?

3 Find a space opposite a partner and face each other. Move together now on the rhythm; for example, press *up* and down, press *up* and down. Keep it going. Can you develop it? How can the movement *grow*?

4 Good. Several people added another idea. Bring in more movements. All practise.

5 Let's make a *big flywheel*. Use big *swings* round and round. The movement begins slowly, then gets faster. Use the right arm, and then the left arm . . . Now slow it down . . .

6 Who can *jump forwards* like a machine gone wrong? Try jerky jumps: jump – jump – jump – and JUMP. Make your *arms* join in.

7 Everyone lie down. Close your eyes. Remember all the different movements we've had. Think about the best ones. Now, with your partner, think how you will begin. Make a short machine dance. Give it a title.

The dance

A partner dance as above. The ideas may be selected from several lessons.

Practising voice sounds

'All sit near me. As I make the up-down piston movement with my arm, you make the sound. When I stop, you stop.' (Have half the class moving a piston arm, half the class sounding.)

In the same way, humming 'circular' sounds, or making *jerky* sounds could be tried.

When the children add sound to their own movement, they can do so quietly, so that the sound accents rather than dominates. It does not need to be loud.

Summary

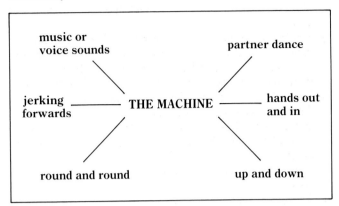

music or voice sounds — partner dance — jerking forwards — THE MACHINE — hands out and in — round and round — up and down

The Machine

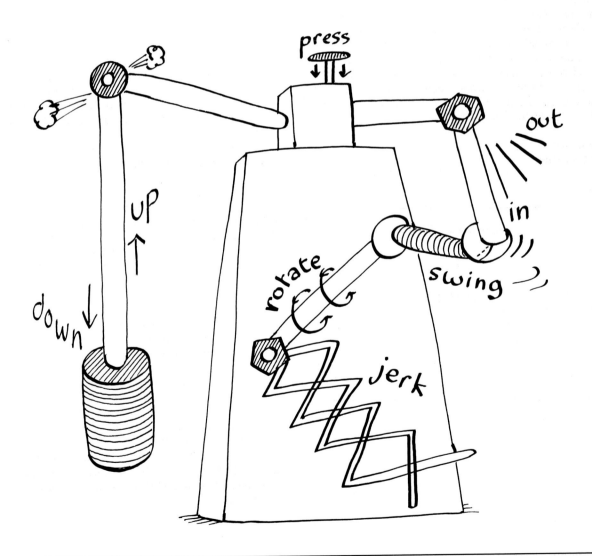

Games

227 'He' or 'Tag'

dodge
freeze

Use 'He' or 'Tag' as a movement framework. Emphasize body parts *dodging* and body shape *stopping*. Organize four groups before the lesson. Do a slow, stretching warm up.

Questions and tasks

1 Sit near me. The first group finds a space in *this half* of the hall. The second group finds a space in the other half of the hall.

2 Both groups have a 'He' person . . . that's you and you. Both groups must stay in their half of the room. When I play the tambour, each groups plays 'He'. When the tambour stops, everyone freezes. Ready . . . Move really fast.

3 Come and sit by me. The third and fourth groups spread out. You do the same thing but I want everyone to move much more. Everyone imagines that they are being chased: dodge one way, the other way, duck down, step to the side. Make it look as if you are all being chased all the time. Imagine . . . When you are touched, you *freeze*. Ready . . .

4 Hold those positions — still. Can you see the different ways they've *stopped* — some high, some low, someone just about to turn, caught in mid-action.

5 (Improving) Everyone find a space. Whichever body *part of you* I call out, move it out of the way in the space, stretch it away as if that is the part that I am going to touch. Ready: Head! Elbow! Knee! Good, some people got themselves in really dramatic positions.

6 Let's make it a slow motion 'He', as if you were being chased in a a dream. Slow motion. Ready . . . move between each other carefully.

7 All try that one. Lean right forward. Good, someone there did a slow-motion swerve to the side.

The dance
Dream 'He'
Two groups move at a time so that the children have plenty of space.
   (a)   Fast-moving 'He', dodging and stopping;
   (b)   Slow-motion 'He', big, slow movements;
   (c)   When touched, slowly collapse to the ground.
Let each group evolve its own idea. Provide the above framework if necessary.

Summary

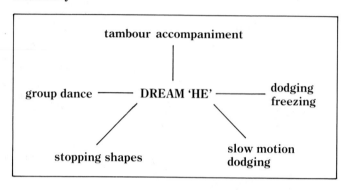

~ OCEAN ~
an exploration in dance and words by
Rosamund Shreeves

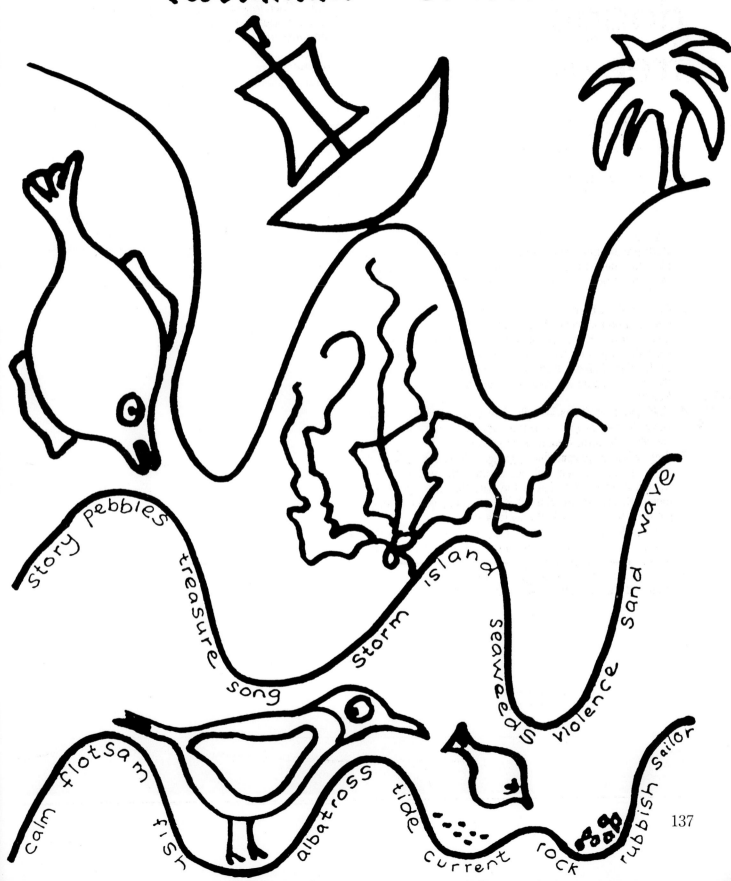

story pebbles treasure song storm island seaweeds violence sand wave

calm flotsam fish albatross tide current rock rubbish sailor

Ocean

Performance for Children

Ocean by Rosamund Shreeves has been performed widely throughout the UK and has been the basis for many children's workshops and residencies in schools. After seeing the performance children were guided to make their own simple performances using dance, words, props, and self-made coloured slides (huge projections on a clear wall of the hall).

Through making their dances and through commenting on and appreciating each other's efforts, the children gained enormously, not only in extending their communication skills, but also in their experience and knowledge of themselves.

Description of the Show

Ocean uses dance ideas from the sea, from the shoreline and from sea creatures, both real and imaginary, and also from our own inner responses to the ocean. Dance is combined with *natural sounds*, the use of *objects* left behind by the tide, and *orginal coloured slides*. The aim is to simulate a powerful sea atmosphere, with its mystery and its scope for play and creativity, that communicates directly through the senses rather than through scientific information. Cartoons and fragments of myth and contemporary story sources are also included.

Although the show is primarily concerned with the identification of the ocean as a source of ideas and energy, questions of what the sea means to us and how we value it for future generations will also be posed.

During the performance these ideas and dances are accompanied by recorded natural sound (electro-acoustic music) by Roger North and on-the-spot accompaniment, using song chants and 'pebble music'.

The performance of *Ocean* includes some participation by children. It could be part of a bigger project. *Ocean* dances arise from ideas of: under the sea, fish, birds, storm, beach objects and pollution.

138

Above: Rosamund Shreeves

Make Your Own Ocean Performance

Suggestions

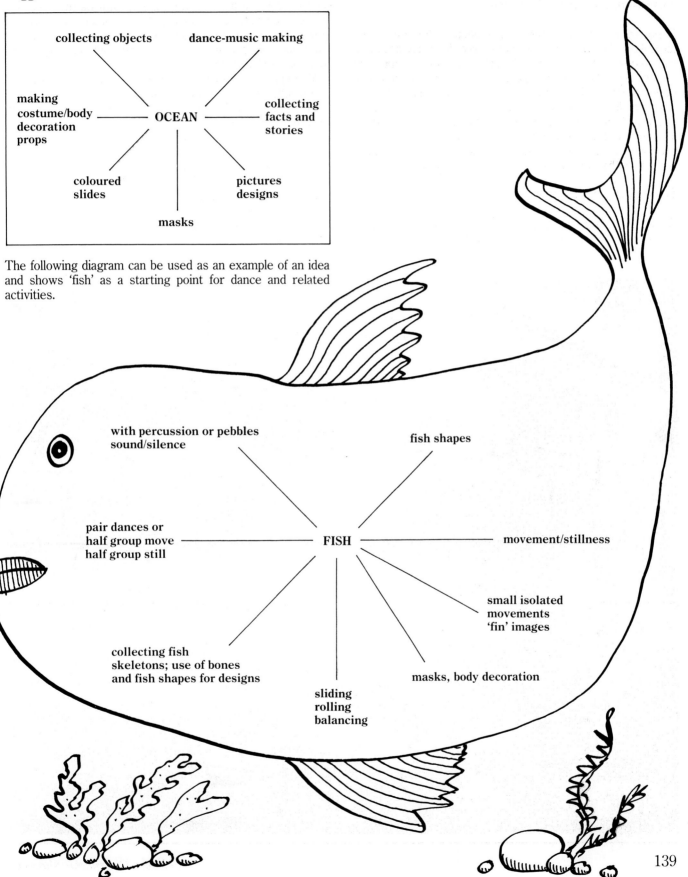

```
                collecting objects       dance-music making

making
costume/body                                          collecting
decoration  ————————  OCEAN  ————————       facts and
props                                                     stories

            coloured                          pictures
             slides                           designs

                        masks
```

The following diagram can be used as an example of an idea and shows 'fish' as a starting point for dance and related activities.

```
    with percussion or pebbles                    fish shapes
    sound/silence

    pair dances or
    half group move  ————————  FISH  ————————  movement/stillness
    half group still

                                                    small isolated
                                                    movements
                                                    'fin' images

    collecting fish
    skeletons; use of bones
    and fish shapes for designs        masks, body decoration

                        sliding
                        rolling
                        balancing
```

The following summaries and brief descriptions are based on actual dances created by children during a residency (i.e. performances of *Ocean* to school children followed by workshops) and give an idea of the sort of simple compositions which children have achieved.

The emphasis was on simplicity, clarity of movement, and on the process of making and presenting a dance, shaped by the choreographer.

The Storm Dance

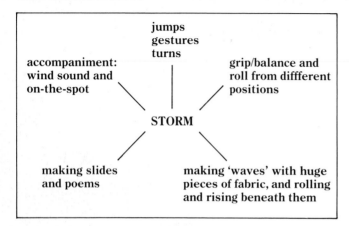

The Dance Form

with/against the wind	The children grouped themselves against the wall becoming 'part of' the projected slide. One by one they were 'blown' from the wall into a space of their own and moved 'with' the wind or resisted it.
sound and poetry	As the wind sound faded they rolled to group around their teacher. Without breaking the flow they began to make soft background sound effects while a few children read their poems.
fabric waves	As the wind grew again, three lots of fabric 'waves' were set in motion and the children dived under them, a few at a time and regrouped against the slide.

My Thoughts

I felt like a leaf being blown off
a tree and I felt as if I were
in a deep sleep and I was sleep walking
in a dream. Then I felt like some
litter blowing out of a bin in the stormy
wind. When I was pushing I felt
as if I was fighting aginst the wind
I felt like a crisp bag being pushed
away in the wind.

When I went near the screen I felt
like a tropical fish with all my pretty
colours on me. When I was spinning
around, I felt like I was an aeroplane
that fell out of the sky.

The Water and Coral Dance

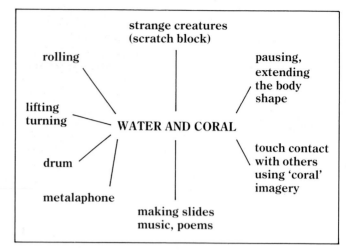

The Dance Form

water	The children began 'on the ocean bed'. The water 'moved them' — rolling, lifting, balancing.
coral	As the sound of the metalaphone changed to the drum-beat, they paused and stretched and 'grew' towards others near them, forming *transient* coral groups, before the water sound began again.
water and coral	The sound pattern of metalaphone music followed by drumming was repeated over and over again and accompanied repeated movement phrases of water and rock movements.
creatures	Then at a signal from the 'scratch block' five children left the coral and travelled as strange creatures, in and out, before returning to the coral and changing places with others. In this way there was a constant interchange of creatures travelling away and back to the still group.
creatures	Then ALL the coral came alive. Everyone was a creature. For a moment, movement everywhere, until . . . They stopped and 'solidified' into strange shapes and groupings, changing back into coral.

Coral

Coral is hard,
Coral is rough,
It sits in the sea like a hard piece of fluff.
It builds up high,
And some grows small,
It sometimes looks round like a ball.
Coral grows jagged and sharp,
Coral is brittle and grows like an arch.
It sometimes is holey,
With some spikes,
And it looks like a tree under the sea.

Right: Rosamund Shreeves

The Island Dance (A polluted island)

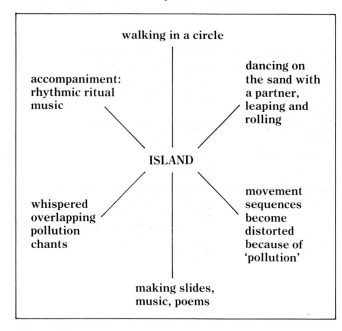

The Dance Form

walking	A ritualized walking in a circle to symbolize the 'island'.
partner dance	A partner dance, fitting in, waiting, following, full of *energy*.
distortion	As the music fades the movement and energy change; some accelerate frantically, some die down.
whispers	Standing, they all turn to face the screen (the projection) and whisper, repeating the 'pollution thoughts', the chant, over and over again. Clear it up. Burn it. Take it away. We don't want it.
falling	One by one, using the same movement, in the same direction, they fall softly to the ground.

The Polluted Island

Waves are drifting by,
Animals are running around,
This is what you call a lovely island.
Everybody is laying in the beautiful delightful sun,
Round us are all the palm trees with their fruit on them.

Poor, poor island. What has happened?
Of all the islands I have seen you are now the worst of all.
Lovely fruit has disappeared.
Lovely things have just gone weird.
Useful fruits you're no good to us now.
Tell the world that this is not happening to us.
I love this island, it is my home.
Oh, I wish we didn't have to leave
No, no, I've left you now.

Making Original Coloured Slides

Materials

1. slide mounts from photography shops
2. clear acetate film from art shops
3. Staedtler Lumocolor pens
4. scissors, white paper, ruler
5. slide projector
6. large white wall.

Cut the acetate to fit the slide mount. Clip the mount together.
Draw your 'ocean' image on the acetate. Using the slide projector, project your image on to the wall. Dance in front of the image.
It will project on to you. Make different images. Use props and music.

Source Reading

Oceans (Paul Hamlyn)
The Book of Water (Benn Ltd)
Pollution of the Sea (Coastal Antipollution League, Alverstoke, Greenway Lane, Bath)
Sea Legends (Hamish Hamilton)

Music List

Bartok	Roumanian Dances etc.	**Mussorgsky**	*Pictures at an Exhibition*
Berlioz	*Roman Carnival Overture*	**Presencer, Alain**	Singing Bowls of Tibet
Bizet	*L'Arlésienne Suite*	**Ravel**	*Mother Goose Suite*
BBC	Sound Effects and Programme Title Music, e.g. *The Flight of the Condor.* Details from BBC Enterprises, Woodlands, 80 Wood Lane, London W12 0TT	**Rossini**	*The Rite of Spring*
		Respighi	
		Saint-Saens	*Carnival of the Animals*
		Satie	*Gymnopedies* etc.
		Simon, Paul	*Gracelands*
Copland	*Rodeo* etc.	**Sousa**	*Marches*
Debussy	Piano Preludes etc.	**Stravinsky**	*The Rite of Spring*
Falla	*El Amor Brujo* etc.	**Sugumugu**	24 Hour Drumming (Stern's Records Live Recording 116 Whitfield Street, London W1)
Flute Music of France	Claudio Records, UK.		
		Vollenweider	*Down to the Moon*
Folk music	Greek, Latin American etc.	**Walton**	*Facade*
Inuit Games and Chants	Philips Records		

More Sources of Music specially for Dance

Benstead, Christopher
Music for Dance. Three tapes with contrasting tracks on a large variety of instruments.
(Music for Dance, PO Box 727, London SE18 3DX)

Menter, Will
Overflow for Children. Music played on unusual instruments.
(Watercatch Farm, Bracknell, Bristol BS19 3EH)

North, Roger
Music for the *Ocean* show and other pieces.
(24 Strand on the Green, London W4 3PH)

Stewart, Ian
Music for Dance and Improvisation. Piano and wide range of live percussion, plus one electronic piece for choreography.
(Flat 30, Quadrant House, Burrell Street, London SE1 0UW)

Woo
Into the Heart of Love. Short tracks of gentle, synthesized music.
(Cloud 9 Music, 39 Abbeygate, Bury St. Edmunds, Suffolk IP33 11W)

Hum Drum Music for Dance
Uses voice, synthesizer, piano and percussion. Pieces suitable for many dance styles.
(14a Station Road, Cullingworth, Bradford, West Yorkshire BD13 5HN)

Useful Sources of Additional Information

The Arts Council of Great Britain
105 Piccadilly,
London W1V 0AU

Dance Pack Guide to Schools which lists addresses, regional arts associations, dance animateurs and small and middle scale dance companies.

The Rambert Dance Company
94 Chiswick High Road
London W4 1SH

Teacher's Pack with video and study notes for children of 12 years and upwards

Chisenhale Dance Space
64/84 Chisenhale Road,
London E3 5QZ

Children's creative dance and youth dance activities

Shreeves, Rosamund
24 Strand on the Green,
London W4 3PH

Dance projects, massage, movement therapy.

National Resource Centre for Dance
The University of Surrey
Guildford
Surrey GU2 5XH